WINCHEE

MISSION STORIES OF COLIN AND MELVA WINCH

SIGNS PUBLISHING
Established 1885

Copyright © 2014 by S Ross Goldstone.

The author assumes full responsibility for the accuracy of all facts and quotations as cited in this book.

Proudly published and printed in Australia by
Signs Publishing
Warburton, Victoria.

This book was
Edited by Nathan Brown
Proofread by Lindy Schneider
Designed by Kym Jackson
Cover and internal photographs provided by Colin and Melva Winch
Cover design by Shane Winfield
Typeset in Berkeley Book 11/14.5

ISBN 978 1 925044 00 3

High Flight

Oh! I have slipped the surly bonds of Earth
And danced the skies on laughter-silvered wings;
Sunward I've climbed, and joined the tumbling mirth
Of sun-split clouds—and done a hundred things
You have not dreamed of—wheeled and soared and swung
High in the sunlit silence. Hov'ring there,
I've chased the shouting wind along, and flung
My eager craft through footless halls of air.

Up, up the long delirious, burning blue,
I've topped the windswept heights with easy grace
Where never lark, or even eagle flew—
And, while with silent, lifting mind I've trod
The high untrespassed sanctity of space,
Put out my hand and touched the face of God.

—Pilot Officer Gillespie Magee
No 412 squadron, Royal Canadian Air Force,
killed December 11, 1941

Foreword

While in army service in New Guinea in the mid-1940s, I first saw the advantage of aeroplanes being used in mission service instead of tediously tramping the muddy mountain trails by foot. A dream developed of becoming a mission pilot—a dream not held by church administration at that time. But, I was soon to learn, it was a dream shared by Colin Winch. Colin and I had no contact until we both became missionaries and we shared the dream, knowing we did not have the support of our leaders.

Through an amazing set of circumstances, I was able to raise funds to buy a new plane and with a change of administration came a change of attitude. Colin and I were delighted. We were the only Seventh-day Adventist missionaries in Papua New Guinea who had pilot licenses, so we were approved to fly the plane. A bond developed between us as we learned the intricate art of flying in a land notorious for its dangerous conditions, where one could expect the unexpected.

We both had 300 hours flying in our logbooks. Colin lived on the coast and I lived in the Highlands, so we agreed he would check my flying on the coast and I would check his in the Highlands. Both areas were hazardous. The coastal airstrips were often covered in long grass and difficult to see until the plane was nearly upon them. Plus it was difficult to avoid the eagles while flying over the low coastal ranges. In the highlands, the short and sometimes steep landing strips were little more than clearings in the tropical jungle, and approaches to them were made more dangerous by the jagged mountains and variable winds. Often as we trained, we would wear a "hood" to limit external visibility and fly by instruments only. This simulated flying in cloud, should we be caught in such conditions while flying through the mountain passes.

There is no-one I would prefer to fly with in the mission fields of the Pacific than Colin Winch. He early set for himself a high standard of excellence, is meticulous in pre-flight checks, is highly skilled in dealing with unexpected flying conditions, and refuses to take unnecessary risks. Best of all, he has a high reliance on our Master Pilot, God our Heavenly Father.

Hats off to you, Col! You are the consummate pilot and I am looking forward to flying with you in the Kingdom Above.

Len Barnard
Pioneer mission pilot

A Leader's Tribute

The first time that I heard the name "Colin Winch" I was serving at the South Pacific Division (SPD) office. I was informed that a nursing student across the road at the Sydney Adventist Hospital was building an aeroplane out of boxes at the rear of the hospital. Of course, we considered it a joke—but the project came from the mind of a young man who wanted to be a pilot.

As the years passed, I was privileged to fly with Colin in different areas of the SPD's mission field. I soon learned that the box plane became a reality for this dedicated young man who wanted to fly for God and to spread the gospel as an angel "flying in the midst of heaven."

We were both appointed as missionaries to the various islands of the South Pacific. Little did I think that our careers would work together in this way. We flew in Papua New Guinea, the Solomon Islands and Vanuatu. We carried personnel to new sites, as well as cargo, including food and other supplies. When on the ground, we preached the Word.

The aviation program was a Divine blessing. When my wife and I went to Port Moresby in 1938, the membership in Papua was 700. Today the combined territory of Papua New Guinea has more than 250,000 church members. We must give great credit to the leading of the Lord in directing the aviation ministry in spreading the staff to pre-war sites and new ones opened up by the war.

We marvel at what Colin, Len Barnard, and other pilots did when led by the Holy Spirit.

Colin always gave me confidence in his ability as a pilot. I often watched him prepare for a flight and no small item was overlooked. I saw him with a small set of scales beside the plane checking everything to ensure he remained within the legal load limit. Colin usually flew a twin-engine plane named the *J L Tucker*, donated to the mission by the Quiet Hour's Tucker family. As well as his regular church duties, Colin flew mercy flights bringing succour to the needy. He gave leadership to the staff of mission pilots, testing them and generally sharing his wisdom. My last flight with Colin was in 1976, when we flew from the Solomons to Vanuatu and beyond.

I thank God for the privilege of being a co-worker with Colin. One could never have wished for a safer pilot. We always worked under the direction of the heavenly angels.

I also pay tribute to Melva—Colin's wife—and the children who spent much time at home waiting for the safe return of their husband and father. As a family, they have been led by the Spirit, and I pray for their ongoing happy retirement and may we all be together in eternity with those whose lives we touched in the South Pacific and beyond.

I shall ever remember the young man who dreamed aviation dreams with wooden boxes and went on to do great things for God.

Robert Frame
Former President (1971–76)
South Pacific Division

Contents

Foreword v
A Leader's Tribute vii

Introduction 1
The Tooth 3
Called to Mission Service 6
The Passion is Born 9
The Call to Kukudu 14
Kukudu 20
Mistaken Enthusiasm 23
Hindi 28
Magic Water 30
The Day the Wharf Fell In 31
Lost at Sea 34
The Queen is Drowned 37
Medical Emergencies 39
Life on a Mission Station 43
Learning to Fly 49
Candidate for the Kalabus 54
Establishing New Airstrips 58
    Another Perspective: 66
The Drop 68
A Tragic Death 72
    Another Perspective: 76
To Go or Not To Go 77
Ama Opening 83
Landing on a Band-aid 93
Foot-slogging Among the Kukukukus 96
Flying Fish and Wandering Feet 101
Search-and-Rescue Missions 103
The Day God Spoke 108
Held Aloft in Angel's Hands 112
Night Flight 118
Heroines of Mission 121
    Another Perspective: 123
Mechanical Difficulties 124

They Heralded the King 127
    Another Perspective: 132
Earthquake 133
A Critical Omission 137
A Presidential Visit 141
    Another Perspective: 144
"Nauru! To the right?" 145
Living With the Unexpected 149
Animals in the Family 153
The Day Nationals Turned White 156
Washing the Angels' Feet 158
Landing Rights and a Broken Wheel 161
Adventure on the Island of Fire 164
Wes Guy: Aviation Mentor 166
The Flying Instructor 171
Chief Pilot 174
    Another Perspective: 177
Family Memories and Reactions 179
"It's a Miracle" 187
Flying With an Angel 191

Afterword 196

Introduction

Colin Morris Winch was born in Toowoomba, Queensland, Australia on July 2, 1932. On completion of his secondary school education, he trained as a nurse at the Sydney Sanitarium and Hospital (now Sydney Adventist Hospital). There he met Melva Franklin, whom he married in November 1955, having received a call to the Amyes Memorial Hospital in the Solomon Islands.

Together, they spent 34 years in the South Pacific islands as nurse, pilot and administrator. Flying was Colin's great passion and, together with Len Barnard, he began the first flying service to the remote villages in Papua New Guinea. This was fraught with great danger due to the mountainous terrain and variable weather conditions. Ever eager for the spread of the gospel to un-entered or remote places, Colin was responsible for encouraging many new airstrips to be built in Papua New Guinea and in the Solomon Islands.

When a twin-engine Aztec aeroplane was donated to the Western Pacific Union Mission, Colin spent many hours in long flights across the vast waters of the Coral Sea and the Pacific Ocean, bringing the gospel to remote islands and atolls, as well as supporting the work of the Seventh-day Adventist church in established communities.

Returning home with his experience and skills as a pilot, Colin was appointed as the first Chief Flying Instructor at the Avondale Flying School, at the same time holding the office of Health Director and Associate Youth Director for the North New South Wales Conference. Later he was appointed Chief Pilot for the South Pacific Division of Seventh-day Adventists, a position he held until 1994.

The love and respect in which Colin and Melva Winch are held throughout the Pacific is indicated by his appointment as president of the Papua New Guinea Union Mission in 1985, president of the Central Pacific Union Mission in 1987, and president of the Western Pacific Union Mission in the mid-1990s—the only missionary to have held the position of president in each of the South Pacific's three union missions.

Winchee

Colin is still in love with flying. He enjoys a game of golf with his friends, but if the day is fine and clear, golf takes second place. Colin will be up in God's heaven, flying with the birds.

These are only some of the stories from Colin and Melva's many years of mission service. But it has been a privilege to hear him re-tell them and to share them with a wider audience.

The Tooth

It was an early morning session at the outpatient clinic at Amyes Memorial Hospital. Colin and Melva had recently arrived in Kukudu and this was one of Colin's first clinic sessions.

The first 10 patients presented with only minor maladies but this changed when Jacob—a large, well-built Solomon Islander with a mop of curly hair—presented, holding his jaw. Assuming he had a tooth problem, Colin seated the patient on the folding dental chair that had been donated by the United States army.

Inspection revealed an excellent mouthful of shiny white teeth but the crown of a huge molar had broken off, creating the discomfort. Colin discovered Jacob had already sought dental treatment from another "doctor" who had failed in his attempt to remove the offending molar and snapped off the crown in the process.

This was to be Colin's first real extraction, the only previous one being at the dental hospital in Sydney and that tooth had almost fallen out of its own volition. He knew this extraction would be a real challenge, even more so since some of the village people would be watching the skill of the new "dentist."

The 24-bed Amyes Memorial Hospital at Kukudu in the Western Solomon Islands.

Winchee

Having prepared a mandibular block, Colin approached Jacob with the gleaming needle at the ready. Jacob knew all about that needle and withdrew his head as Colin endeavoured to inject the anaesthetic.

Lakana—the clinic assistant—sensed the problem and positioned himself behind the patient. Grabbing Jacob's hair with powerful hands, he said, *"Shoot him, Doctor! Mi passim pinis!"* ("Give the injection! He won't move now!")

To make sure of deadening the area, Colin injected the anaesthetic into the gum beside the tooth as well. While waiting for the anaesthetic to take effect, Colin noticed the audience below the clinic windows, listening to the commentary provided by the observers at the door. The outpatients were curious to know whether the new "Doctor" could be trusted as a dentist.

Selecting the lower-jaw forceps, Colin approached the apprehensive patient. With Lakana continuing to hold Jacob by the hair, Colin planted his feet firmly on the floor, gripped the molar, squeezed and pulled, pushed, levered and pulled again.

The tooth did not move! Failure as a "dentist" had become a real possibility. Eating coconut and native foods had made for strong teeth.

The day was hot and steamy. Any ventilation that might have reached Colin had been blocked by the curious and excited spectators relaying a commentary to those who could not see. There were beads of perspiration on Colin's brow—also on Jacob's, although for different reasons.

Colin selected alternative American-donated forceps and gripped the offending tooth once more. Jacob sank deeper into the chair, restrained by Lakana. Pull! Push! Pull!

It seemed like an hour Colin worked on that tooth without success. Some of the observers were beginning to have doubts! Others were beginning to leave, deciding the new "dentist" was no good.

Then Jacob said, "Doctor, you have forgotten something!"

"No! I don't think so, Jacob," he replied. Colin checked the sterile tray. All was in order.

"You have forgotten to pray, Doctor!"

Incredulous at his own forgetfulness, Lakana and Colin helped Jacob out of the dental chair and the three of them knelt in prayer. The spectators whispered the news. "They are praying!"

The Tooth

Expectations rose again. Some of those who were about to leave decided to stay to observe the answer to prayer.

Back in the chair, Jacob received another pain-deadening injection. Taking up the same pair of forceps, Colin offered another silent prayer and, placing his feet firmly on the floor once more, gripped the molar and pulled.

Those four huge, curled molar roots came out as easily as pulling a nail out of soft timber. "It's out!" went up the cry as Colin held up the offending tooth. In his excitement, Lakana had failed to loosen his grip on Jacob's hair. But, with an enormous grin and blood dribbling from his mouth, Jacob praised God for the miracle.

So did Colin. His reputation was intact and his dental practice began to flourish.

Called to Mission Service

Growing up in Concord, an inner-western suburb of Sydney and attending the local Seventh-day Adventist Church, an old German sawmiller, Fred Ludwig, formed a friendship with young Colin, constantly encouraging him to set his sights on becoming a missionary. "Vun day you vill be a meesionary!" he would say.

Seeds were being planted and these would be well watered. As an early teenager, Colin attended a church regional meeting in the Assembly Hall near Wynyard Station in central Sydney. The guest speaker was Dr Joers, a medical practitioner from South Africa.

Gripped by the stories told by this missionary, Colin's heart was stirred and he became convicted, as never before, to dedicate his life to becoming a medical missionary. At the end of the sermon, the doctor made an appeal for those who would dedicate their lives to mission service to leave their seats, walk to the front and meet with him for a prayer of dedication. Colin was under deep conviction. He wanted to respond, but being "pathologically shy" he was riveted to his seat, fear gripping his heart.

No-one responded.

The doctor made a second appeal. Again a trembling Colin felt compelled to respond but again fear of making a show of himself in front of 600 people held him back. Finally, when the third appeal was made, Colin knew that God had spoken to him and he could resist no longer.

Leaving his seat, on trembling legs, with pounding heart and dryness of mouth, he made his way to the front. A dedicatory prayer offered by the missionary doctor sealed in Colin's mind the determination to

Called to Mission Service

become a medical missionary. It was God's will for his life.

Colin did not come from an academic family. An average student while attending the Burwood Adventist High School, he struggled hard to achieve academic success, studying up to seven hours a day for his Leaving Certificate. Allan Jones, a fellow student in his class, was also interested in medicine and when both achieved good passes sufficient to receive scholarships, he urged Colin to join him in studying at university to become a doctor.

Colin would have loved to do so, but believed Jesus would return before he completed the seven years of training. Instead, he decided a shorter four-year course at the Sydney Sanitarium and Hospital would be a viable alternative and would allow him to apply for mission service at an earlier date.

* * *

Being six months short of the minimum entry age to the nursing course, Colin applied for and received a position as storeman with the Sanitarium Health Food Company. This involved delivery work, driving the Sanitarium truck to various shops around Sydney, to the Walsh Bay wharf, and to the Interstate and Country Rail Depot at Darling Harbour.

Deliveries to the rail depot were difficult due to the random location of wagons for country stations. They were seldom in the same location. New Australian staff, who were supposed to assist with unloading, proved reluctant to do so until Colin hit on the idea of carrying with him company "seconds" that he would give to those who assisted him in his work. Soon the word spread and the staff became very co-operative when the Sanitarium truck arrived.

"Vere are you going, Col-in?" they would ask.

"Tamworth."

"Eet is zis one heer!"

In no time, the truck was unloaded and Colin was on his way back to the depot, leaving behind a jar of Marmite, a packet of Weet-Bix or a container of honey.

What had proved successful at the railway sheds was to prove equally effective with the wharf workers at Walsh Bay. Inevitably, there were lengthy delays in having the truck unloaded onto pallets for overseas shipping. One could wait as long as two days. On one occasion, Colin arrived in the unloading bay at the time of the afternoon break. While the men sipped their tea, young Colin began to unload his tins of honey. That was until a heavy hand was placed on his shoulder and a huge "Wharfie" spun him around, looked him in the eye and said with a threatening tone, "Don't you do our work, son!"

The next time Colin arrived at Walsh Bay wharf, he brought with him an assortment of Sanitarium products, all rejects but in perfectly good order. On arrival, he found he was Number 20 in the queue. Taking samples of the products with him, Colin proceeded to the office of the Clerk of Works, gifted him the products and said, "There is more for the men if you can expedite the unloading!"

Within five minutes, there was a shrill whistle. Looking up, Colin could see the Clerk of Works standing at the gate and yelling through cupped hands, "Sanitarium! You are cleared to come!" On pulling out of the queue, Colin passed a number of other waiting vehicles. Within five minutes of entering, his truck was unloaded!

In many ways, this transition period was a God-send because a shy teenager learned how to meet people—all types of people. Gradually, Colin's confidence increased and he lost some of his shyness. God was preparing him for service in the "real" world.

The Passion is Born

Doug Ling, Ellis Gibbons and Colin Winch were bored! Off duty, they sat in Colin's room in the nurses' residence at the Sydney Sanitarium and Hospital, wondering what they could do.

"Why don't we build an aeroplane?" said Colin

"Why a plane?" the others responded. "We know nothing about planes. Do you mean a model plane?"

"No! A real plane that flies!"

The idea was tossed around and finally consensus was reached. They would build an aeroplane.

Knowing nothing about building aeroplanes, they decided to visit the New South Wales State Library and find material on the task ahead. Doug and Colin made the trip into Sydney, and found their way to the library with its shelves stacked with books. Never had they seen so many books.

They peered through the glass doors, drawing the attention of a bespectacled lady seated at the desk. Opening the doors, the boys went to speak to her.

"Can I help you?" the woman asked.

"We are wanting to find a book on how to build an aeroplane," replied Colin, the designated spokesman. Directing the two trainee nurses to the card system, the librarian suggested that they look up "Aeronautics."

After a process of searching, they located some books and began to read. The technical nature of the information made no sense to them.

Finally Doug said, "Why don't we just measure the wing span in comparison to the body? Then it will be OK."

So that is what they took back to Wahroonga—only measurements!

Winchee

Ellis was the owner of a bandsaw, located below the dormitory. Doug was skilled at wood carving, so he was responsible for creating the wings. And Colin was given the task of obtaining timber.

Colin drove to a timber mill on the outskirts of the Sydney suburb of Hornsby. Speaking to the foreman, he asked about the availability of seasoned, light but cheap timber.

"What do you need it for?" asked the foreman.

At first reluctant to reveal their purpose, Colin finally revealed that it was for the construction of an aeroplane.

The foreman shook his head in disbelief. "There is a heap of old timber down the back," he said. "Help yourself."

So Colin returned with lengths of timber hanging out the windows of his old Chrysler car.

"We have the timber," he announced to his co-builders. "Now we have to obtain some sort of fabric to cover the wings."

Another Hornsby visit resulted in a free bolt of water-damaged cotton fabric sufficient to clad the wooden framework.

None of the builders had ever been near a plane to see the internal workings of an aeroplane, so the end result was primitive, particularly when Doug decided to shorten the wingspan in comparison to the size of the body. The fuselage was made just wide enough to house Colin's slender frame.

News of the venture had spread throughout the hospital, resulting in the young male nurses copping a good deal of banter from their female associates. "It will never get off the ground," they taunted.

"You wait and see," responded a confident Colin. "Soon we'll be circling around the San, and you'll be there waving to us!"

Of course, the plane had to have an undercarriage but even this problem was quickly solved. There was a pram lying under the old wooden hospital building. This was commandeered and put to good use.

Eventually the time came for the maiden flight. One Sunday morning, the fuselage was loaded onto the back of a small truck and transported to Turramurra Park. To reach the park, they passed the local Catholic church as worshippers attended morning mass. Their curiosity aroused, some followed the vehicle to the park, not wanting to miss out on the

The Passion is Born

excitement. A second trip brought the wings and the plane was bolted together.

Colin had assumed he would be the pilot. After all, he had built the bodywork just wide enough for him to sit in—and besides, he had a driver's licence!

But Doug had other ideas. "I built the wings, therefore I should have the first flight!" he argued.

Eventually, a coin was tossed and Doug won. Then a real problem arose. How was a rather more portly Doug to fit into the space built only to house a slender Colin?

With much squeezing and pushing while Catholic onlookers held the plane secure, Doug was compressed into the pilot's seat. A rope was attached to the front of the plane with the other end held by Colin seated on the back of the truck and the signal given to the driver to accelerate.

A look of fear crossed Doug's face as the plane rumbled its way across the turf. He was heading for brick houses and trees. But what would happen if the plane did actually take off?

Amateur aircraft builders Douglas Ling (left) and Colin standing by their creation in Turramurra Park, Sydney, before the first test flight in 1955.

Winchee

"Pull the stick back! Pull the stick back!" shouted Colin in an attempt to achieve lift off.

In vain! There was no lift and the towing vehicle was heading for a deep ditch, previously unseen by the prospective aviators. Sensing the danger, the driver swung violently to avoid the obstacle but the plane held its line, coming to rest just short of the ditch.

With great effort and groans of pain, an effort was made to extricate Doug from the fuselage. They lifted and tugged but only lifted the whole plane from the ground. The onlookers ran to give assistance, holding the plane down while the extraction proceeded. It was like pulling a molar from a human jaw—without painkillers! Eventually he was freed and it was decided to make a second attempt, this time with Colin as pilot.

The truck driver suggested that a longer runway could be achieved by cutting across the park at a different angle. The second attempt began, this time with Colin in the plane and Doug on the back of the truck.

All was well until they reached a slightly elevated cricket pitch. As the pram wheels hit the small mound, there was a bang and the undercarriage was ripped away. Then Colin noted that the rumbling had ceased and he was suspended in air.

He was flying!

After coming to rest, Colin emerged from the plane. "It flew! It flew!" he enthused. "How far off the ground were we?"

The others confirmed the plane had in fact flown—a full 6 inches (15 centimetres) above the ground.

Assured that flight was possible, the plane was returned to Wahroonga where alterations were made and the undercarriage lowered and strengthened, turning it into an improvised glider.

Because of a lack of transport, it was decided that the next attempt should be made in one of the cow paddocks on the hospital farm. George Evans owned an early-model Chevvy with a seat at the back. When all was in readiness, Colin climbed into the now-widened pilot seat at the front of the plane and George accelerated away, hurtling down the paddock.

As they gained speed, they realised cows had recently been feeding in the paddock and wet cow dung was being thrown up all over Colin.

The Passion is Born

Desperately, he called a halt and cleaned the offending manure from his face and hair.

Then it was Doug's turn and he, too, was covered in fresh cow manure.

There was only one thing to do: let the plane fly without a pilot.

Once more, George hurtled down the paddock in his car—and the plane took off! Round and round the paddock drove George. Fifteen feet (almost 5 metres) above him, the plane flew in hot pursuit. For its young builders, it was a thing of beauty.

It is one thing to fly a plane; it is another thing to land it.

"Slow down, George—slowly," called Colin.

As George slowed down, the plane caught up and threatened to crash into the back of his car. In grave danger, George accelerated away. By this time, Colin was running alongside the vehicle calling out again, "Slow down, George—slowly!"

Every time George slowed his car, the plane threatened to crash into him. In desperation, he headed for a tree and swerved away at the last minute, allowing the plane to end its flight, a crumpled heap of junk—never to fly again.

The plane died an ignominious death—but the love of flying was forever implanted in Colin's heart. Soon two loves would be linked: a love of flying and mission service.

The Call to Kukudu

"Brother Winch! There is a call for you to the Western Solomon Islands to become the Superintendent of the Amyes Memorial Hospital at Kukudu. Will you accept the appointment?"

Colin was jumping for joy. The many letters he had written to the Australasian Division secretary informing him of his yearning to be a medical missionary had at last borne fruit. Not only was Colin now a Registered Nurse, he had also been studying diesel engines and ship's navigation to prepare himself for a life of service in a mission field somewhere in the Pacific. There was one problem, however. He was a single man—and unmarried men were not accepted for mission service.

Melva Franklin had never planned to marry. She and her sister, Phyllis, had decided to set up an orphanage and devote their lives to caring for children. Encouraged by her father to leave school at an early age, Melva spent five years employed as a domestic in the Horsham

Sisters, Phyllis and Melva, as student nurses training at the Sydney Sanitarium in 1953.

The Call to Kukudu

Hospital until she received a letter from Phyllis, encouraging her to apply for the nursing course at the Sydney Sanitarium and Hospital.

Not having completed her secondary school education, Melva was required to sit examinations in English and mathematics prior to official acceptance into the course. Success in these exams ensured Melva's acceptance and she joined her sister in training as a nurse.

At the hospital, Colin and his friends had developed a reputation as pranksters. Sometimes his escapades resulted in him being called before the faculty and disciplined. On one such occasion, he and Doug Ling were placed on dishwashing duties, a disciplinary action for which both young men were grateful. It gave them opportunity to meet some lovely first-year nurses, one of whom was Melva.

As the resulting friendship developed into courtship and eventually to talk of marriage, Melva's dreams of caring for children in an orphanage began to fade. She became aware of Colin's commitment to mission service and gave him her full support.

But Melva was not jumping for joy when Colin informed her of his call to Kukudu and that he must go as a married missionary. She had her heart set on finishing her final year of training. Happy for Colin but deeply disappointed at the prospect of not finishing her chosen course, she said "Yes" when Colin proposed to her in August, 1955. They had discussed marriage prior to the call, but Melva had not anticipated it would come so early in her training. Colin was well aware of her turmoil but proudly pointed out the opportunity that had come their way. He was to be the superintendent of a mission hospital!

So Melva put aside her own ambitions. After all, "a promise is a promise"—and they were married by Pastor Ralph Wood on November 22, 1955, in the Horsham church in country Victoria. With excitement mounting, they made the final preparations for their departure from Australia. This included Colin doing intensive training in both anaesthetics and dentistry, and Melva spending six weeks in the maternity ward at the San.

Keen to learn as much as he could about every aspect of medicine, Colin took every opportunity to observe the skills of Dr Allan Tullock (surgeon) and Dr John Letham (anaesthetist).

One day, Colin was in the operating theatre's observation gallery and

Winchee

was noticed by Dr Letham. Knowing Colin had been appointed to Amyes Memorial Hospital, he called out in a loud voice, "Winch! You had better get down here and learn how to give an anaesthetic!"

Never one to knock back an opportunity, Colin scrubbed up, put on

Colin and Melva's wedding portrait taken at Horsham, Victoria, on November 22, 1955.

mask, boots and gown, and presented himself at the operating table. Fortunately, the patient was drowsy from the pre-operative medication and unaware that a beginner was about to administer anaesthetics. However, Dr Tullock was well aware of what was happening. This was his patient and he knew the risks involved. Fortunately—and to Colin's great relief—everything went well and the surgery was completed successfully.

Extracting teeth was a major task for every medical missionary, so Colin was sent to the Sydney Dental Hospital to undergo a crash course in dentistry. Dressed in a white coat like all the other trainees, he spent a week observing experienced dentists going about their profession.

Finally, he was given the task of extracting an elderly patient's tooth. Opening his mouth, the patient indicated the offending tooth.

"This one?" Colin asked, touching the tooth.

There was no need of reply. The tooth was so loose it that fell out of its own accord. A successful extraction, but hardly adequate to prepare the young missionary for the days ahead.

* * *

Finally January 17, 1956, arrived—the day of their departure from Australia. It was a day of great excitement, particularly for Colin. Not only was he beginning a life of mission service, but he was to board a real aeroplane, something he had always dreamed about.

Melva reacted somewhat differently. She was leaving family and friends behind, with no guarantee she would ever see them again. In those days, mission service was for life. This had been emphasised repeatedly by church leaders. There was sadness mingled with apprehension: apprehension about flying; apprehension about her inexperience as a midwife; apprehension about a new and strange culture; apprehension about not having access to shops. After all, she had never been taught to cook. How could she possibly cope without the necessary ingredients being readily available? All of these thoughts and more flashed through her mind as the Australasian Division driver drove them from the Wahroonga mission flats to the international airport in Sydney.

Apprehension about flying and motion sickness was easily cared

Winchee

for. A motion sickness tablet cared for that so well that when the DC6 aeroplane landed in Brisbane for refuelling she could not be wakened, so the cabin crew left her on board to sleep it off.

The new missionaries were soon introduced to the unexpected and bizarre happenings of their chosen vocation. In transit, they spent a longer-than-planned stopover in a vacant mission house in Lae. It was well elevated with shower facilities at ground level. On going downstairs to have a shower, Melva was horrified to find toads jumping all over the place, including in the shower room itself. It was a rude shock to such a new and innocent missionary—and an emotional challenge.

To Colin it was one great adventure! Of course, such experiences became commonplace later in their years of service, but for the uninitiated it was somewhat daunting.

The 45-foot (14-metre), wooden-hulled *Varivato* lay at anchor about 100 feet (30 metres) from the Barakoma airstrip, waiting to take Colin and Melva to their post of duty. Painted white with green trim and sleek lines, the boat was a thing of splendour on that hot, humid tropical morning.

They were welcomed aboard by the native captain, Irwin Harvey

The *MV Varivato* at the wharf near the hospital at Kukudu.

The Call to Kukudu

(headmaster of the Kukudu School) and a tall, noble-looking Solomon Islander with a huge crop of tightly-curly hair. His infectious smile revealed a set of shining white teeth. It was none other than Kata Rangoso himself. Floating on the deep waters of the Coral Sea, Colin could not help but marvel at the beauty of their surroundings.

Having heard that the young couple's freight had arrived, the captain set sail for Gizo. It was a glorious morning and a calm sea. Suddenly there was a cry from the bow: "*Masa! Egat sumpela pis istap along boat. U kam lookim!*"

Bottle-nosed dolphins were frolicking in the bow wave of the boat. Colin and Melva stood in the bow, holding on to the rail as they watched these marvellous creatures playing in the crystal-clear water. Never having seen dolphins before, Colin and Melva felt as if they were in heaven.

However, to their disappointment, on arrival at Gizo they found their freight had not yet arrived. At the advice of Irwin, the newlyweds visited some of the Chinese corrugated-iron stores in Gizo, procuring basic grocery supplies prior to the *Varivato* making the 90-minute crossing to Kukudu and their first home together!

Kukudu

Excitement mounted as the *Varivato* approached Kolombagara Island and the Kukudu Mission Station. Colin and Melva stood on the bow of the boat gazing at the sight before them. They noted the cone-shaped 6000-foot (1800-metre) extinct volcano that dominated the island. The blue waters of the ocean rose and fell right up to the coconut-palmed shoreline. There was no harbour to enter. Instead, the captain steered the ship toward an indented coastline from which a wharf projected into the sea.

The Amyes Memorial Hospital came into view among the coconut palms and slightly elevated above the shoreline. Beyond it and slightly more elevated was the doctor's residence. Both were in need of a coat of paint.

Across a stream was the school and the Harveys' residence. In the centre was the Western Solomons Mission office and what appeared to be a large church. With its tree-clad mountain backdrop, the scene was certainly idyllic on a beautiful afternoon. The more Colin saw of this tropical paradise, the more he fell in love with it.

"Thank you, God, for giving us the joy of serving You in this glorious place," he prayed.

They were only a little way from the wharf when their attention was drawn to a happy crowd of Solomon Islanders gathered to meet the new "Doctor" and his wife. The curious crowd included older folk, women with babies on the hip, tall strong men with muscular frames, young men and girls, and children from the school—all with big smiles, shining white teeth, "fuzzy-wuzzy" hair and ebony bodies. It seemed the whole community had gathered in welcome.

A long line was formed and as the handsome new "Doctor" and the somewhat more shy bride alighted from the boat, the welcoming handshakes began. The line seemed to go on forever until finally Melva said, "Haven't we seen that face before?" This man had a toothless grin and an unusual gait, thus standing out from the crowd. They realised

Kukudu

people were doubling back for a second—and sometimes third—handshake and a look at the new arrivals.

The Harveys kindly took Colin and Melva into their home as the new missionaries' pre-shipped belongings had not yet arrived. Not having received any cross-cultural training, Melva was grateful for this opportunity for a deeper understanding of what lay before her and to learn new housekeeping skills.

Colin cast his appreciative eyes over their wonderful location. He noted the manicured grassy compound with pathways, linking all the main buildings, lined with Croton bushes. The pink and red flowers added a splash of colour to the greens of the grass and coconut palms. He determined to paint the hospital and doctor's residence so that their fresh clean appearance would match nature's beauty and make it into a model mission station.

There was to be no rest, however, for the new hospital superintendent. Colin was soon called on for his medical expertise.

Melva standing in front of the old doctor's house at Amyes Memorial Hospital. This was the Winch's first mission home.

Winchee

Late on their first night, Colin heard the patter of feet on the ladder to the verandah. The visitor knocked and Irwin Harvey went to answer the door.

Melva woke and Colin said to her, "I have a feeling that I am about to have my first patient."

A moment later, Irwin knocked softly on the door. "Colin, are you awake?" he asked. "They need you over at the hospital."

When Colin left the verandah, he realised he had not thought to borrow a torch. He tried to walk over the unfamiliar path and then remembered there was a stream to cross and the bridge had been built haphazardly, changing directions in several places.

A couple of times, Colin's foot missed the planking altogether and he was in danger of tumbling into the stream below. Fortunately, with no-one around to see, he dropped to his knees and crawled across the bridge until he reached the other side.

Eventually, Colin stumbled into the hospital. A patient was vomiting copious amounts of blood and coughing furiously. Colin ordered medication to stop the bleeding and asked for ice. None was available. The large kerosene refrigerator containing the medicines was up at the doctor's residence—and didn't work anyway!

The next morning the patient was transported on the *Varivato* to the government hospital in Gizo and admitted. Unfortunately, he died a few days later.

It was an inauspicious start to Colin's career as a medical missionary.

The hospital staff nurses, with Lekizoto (fourth from the left) and Head Nurse, Lakana (last on the right).

Mistaken Enthusiasm

It is inevitable that inexperienced missionaries will make mistakes in cross-cultural ministry in their enthusiasm to change lives with the gospel. Colin was no exception.

It was a hot, steamy Sabbath afternoon and Colin asked Lakana—the chief national doctor boy—to take him and Melva to the small Hansenide Colony where as many as 12 lepers resided.

Colin knew a little about leprosy, having spent a week at Sydney University studying tropical diseases. His reading of the Bible had made him aware that leprosy was considered a highly infectious disease in Bible times. To his surprise, he had learned that it was no longer considered highly contagious and that appropriate drugs could arrest the progress of the disease.

While Colin may have relayed this information to Melva, her reaction to close contact with this horrible disease was still based on the information found in the Bible. One does not change long-established thinking overnight. Consequently, she was most apprehensive as she accompanied her husband and Lakana down the beautiful Croton-lined road to the colony.

Colin shared his wife's apprehension but was determined to demonstrate compassion and acceptance—and to change the islanders' reaction to leprosy. When he informed Melva that he was going to shake hands with the lepers and wanted her to do so also, Melva was terrified. She thought such an act could curtail their mission service and possibly leave them with the same hideous physical disfigurement they were seeking to counteract. The professor had said that the disease was no longer considered "highly contagious." That did not deny that it

Winchee

was contagious under certain circumstances! While she admired Colin's determination to change attitudes, she doubted the wisdom of what he was about to do.

On arrival, the newly arrived missionaries noted the beautiful white-painted houses with their thatched roofs, neatly laid out on each side of the clearing. They also noted a little thatched chapel at one end of the clearing, and a dispensary and surgery down by the beach. At the entrance to the compound, they were met by the head leper—Ronnie—who greeted them in impeccable English: "Mr and Mrs Winch, I welcome you to the Solomon Islands and to our humble home!"

Colin moved forward and, to Ronnie's surprise, held out his hand. "Ronnie! I want to shake your hand!" he said.

Ronnie was confused! He knew this was taboo. He was not permitted to touch a "clean" person. Now it seemed this new "doctor" missionary really wanted to shake hands. Ronnie extended his hand and, with a beaming Solomon Island smile, shook Colin's hand.

Lakana was shocked! He had never shaken a leper's hand, except

Head Leper, Ronnie, presenting Melva and Colin with two walking sticks, which he himself carved, as a welcoming present.

Mistaken Enthusiasm

when wearing a surgical glove. What was this crazy white man doing? His information about leprosy was also based on Bible times.

Melva cringed. She knew what was coming.

"Honey!" said Colin, "Would you like to shake Ronnie's hand also?"

With fear in her eyes but a smile on her face, Melva stepped forward and shook the hand.

Then it happened.

The other lepers had seen the drama unfold. Rushing down the pathways, they greeted the missionaries, extending their hands to be shaken. Some had no fingers, others were limping on toeless feet—but, with only one exception, they all joined in the joyful greeting.

The one exception was a woman, Bare by name, endeavouring to hide behind a coconut palm near her cottage.

"Let's go over and greet this lady!" Colin said to Melva.

With the wisdom of a woman's instinct, Melva tried to discourage her husband from doing so. In his sincere desire to identify with the lepers, showing he had no fear of defilement, this new missionary failed to listen to the wisdom of his wife and persisted with his intention.

Putting on his best welcoming smile, he approached the poor woman and said, "Bare, I would like to shake hands with you."

The church and residents' cottages at the leper colony near Kukudu.

Winchee

Her eyes were on the ground as she slunk further around the tree. Still Colin persisted, following her around the tree until, finally, with a shamed expression on her lowered face, she extended the stump of her arm to him.

She had no hands! Shocked, Colin shook her arm and retreated to the chapel, chagrined and mortified. He had caused emotional hurt to the poor woman. A great lesson had been learned.

* * *

Medical care of the lepers involved monthly testing of tissue taken from earlobes to determine the presence of bacillus in the surface tissue. If the tests proved clear over a three-month period, the delighted patient was permitted to leave the colony and return home. Conversely there was great disappointment should the tests show the ongoing presence of bacillus.

Colin was responsible for carrying out these tests and so became intimately aware of the emotional fluctuations of the lepers. While studying tropical diseases at Sydney University, he was made aware of the importance of trimming the lesions' edges in order to allow good tissue to fill in and heal the sore. Lakana advised Colin of these weekly procedures, which he demonstrated in the surgical room at the Kukudu Hansenide Clinic.

Leprosy affects the nerves, particularly of peripheral areas such as fingers and toes, resulting in no sensation of pain in such affected areas. The fingers may be burnt by contact with a hot cooking pot or the toes stubbed on a rock. In such cases the leper is unaware of any damage done unless there is the smell of burning flesh or blood seeps from the wound. As a result, sores form and the infection eats away at the appendages.

To Colin's horror, Lakana administered no local anaesthetic but proceeded to remove the affected flesh with a bone nibbler. Colin was horrified and nauseated but the patient exhibited no discomfort and often carried on an animated conversation about some planned activity for later in the day. There were outbursts of laughter as stories were shared or jokes told as the wound was trimmed. It was a strange, new, and unsettling experience for Colin to observe.

Mistaken Enthusiasm

When some of the lesions did not respond, it was decided to invite Dr Scott, a young British doctor based at Gizo Public Hospital, to visit the clinic and perform surgery on the worst-affected feet. Colin was to administer anaesthetics. While he had witnessed many operations and on one occasion had even anaesthetised one of Dr Tullock's patients under the supervision of Dr Letham, Colin had never administered open ether.

The first patient, Jeremiah, was to have surgery and was given a pre-med some 40 minutes prior to being wheeled into the very basic theatre. The drowsy Jeremiah was placed on the operating table where Colin placed the mask over the patient's nose and mouth and began to administer the anaesthetic. When it was deemed the leper was sufficiently anaesthetised, Colin gave the signal for surgery to commence. Blowflies, with obvious intentions, frantically buzzed on the screened windows, attempting to enter the "cutting room."

Dr Scott began to make the necessary incisions but Jeremiah's foot moved. "He is a bit light, Col," said the surgeon. "Give him more ether!" Completing a neat flap across the bottom of the foot, Dr Scott covered what had been a large lesion.

When stitching had been completed and dressings applied, Colin lightened the anaesthetic. Slapping his patient gently on the cheek, Colin said, "Wake up. Jeremiah. It is all over!"

Jeremiah's eyes flashed open and exclaimed *"Hausat yu tok wak up! Mi no savi slip yet!"* (Wake up? I haven't slept yet!)

The hot and humid climate had caused much of the ether to evaporate before Jeremiah had a chance to inhale it. Dr Scott suggested that maybe Colin should give a lot more ether to the next patient.

The chagrined medic was happy to comply.

Hindi

When Colin and Melva accepted an appointment to Kukudu, Melva realised that one of her responsibilities would be that of midwifery. With this in mind, she spent her final three months of nursing training in the obstetrics ward at the Sydney Sanitarium and Hospital. This gave her the opportunity to observe all facets of birth, care of mothers and their babies. However, during this time she was not given opportunity to deliver any babies. This soon changed when she arrived at Kukudu.

Culture plays an important part in the lives of every ethnic group and this was true throughout these islands with regard to the birthing of babies. Babies were not born in the village or in the presence of males. Each village would build a birthing hut or garden house in an area removed from the main residential area.

When a birth was about to take place, the mother-to-be would retire to the birthing hut where she would be attended by other females from the village. After the birth, mother and baby may spend some days or even weeks in the birthing hut. As Western culture spread throughout the islands and medical facilities were provided, clinics, hospital beds or obstetric units took the place of the traditional birthing huts and mothers-to-be made their way to these more modern facilities.

Kukudu had a small obstetric unit independent of the hospital, located near the medical superintendent's house. It was in this facility that Melva gained her experience in delivering babies—more than 100 of them.

One birth caused particular concern. After two days of labour endured by the mother, it was decided that the woman should be transferred to Gizo where she could be under the care of a qualified doctor. Women were reluctant even for male doctors to attend them during childbirth, but would submit to the situation provided the doctor was qualified.

The *Varivato* was docked at the wharf, so Melva asked that the pregnant woman be placed on a stretcher and carried by female staff to the wharf—a five-minute walk. On arrival, the mother-to-be suddenly cried out, *"Emi kum now!"* ("The child is coming!")

Colin heard the commotion and then the silence. Looking up from what he was doing on the boat, he noted that all men had disappeared and attention was being focused on him. He realised his presence was not welcome. One of the nurses explained that custom required all males to be absent and he was asked to leave.

He distanced himself with the other men and left Melva to care for the delivery.

Kneeling on the rough-hewn timber decking did not make for the easiest delivery. Amid cries of pain could be heard, *"Pusim long"* ("Keep pushing") and *"Pusim strong"* ("Push hard").

In due course, Melva heralded the arrival of a baby boy who was later named "Hindi" meaning "Born on a wharf."

It was another cultural learning experience for the new missionaries.

Kukudu's rough-hewn wharf where Melva delivered Hindi.

Magic Water

While at Kukudu, Colin patrolled throughout many of the islands of the Western Solomons, carrying with him vital medicines with which he treated church members and non-church members alike. Often patients presented with dental problems requiring extractions.

On one occasion, a man presented with an aching tooth, requesting to have it taken out. Having run out of anaesthetics, Colin informed the man he could not extract the offending tooth as it would be extremely painful to do so. Sick of the nagging ache, the gentleman insisted he would rather put up with short-term severe pain than continue with the nagging pain. Reluctantly, Colin agreed to extract the tooth and, getting a number of men to hold the patient, he proceeded to relieve the patient of his problem. With a grin of gratitude, the brave man headed home with blood trickling from his lips.

* * *

Penicillin was the marvel of the age. Fortunately, the United States Army had, on departure at the end of World War II, donated large supplies to mission clinics and hospitals. Just one injection of oily penicillin was often sufficient to deal with a medical problem. As a result, these medical clinics were well attended.

Colin noticed that some patients presented claiming minor complaints such as a headache, and expecting to be given an injection. On examination, there was no discernible illness, with the "patient" hoping for an injection just in case at some future time he or she might get sick.

Fortunately, the US Army had also donated large supplies of triple-distilled water, a gift for which there was little medicinal use. Colin decided to "treat" these patients with an injection of distilled water. Such injections stung considerably—a factor that convinced the nationals it was "good medicine." It seems the more it stung the better the medicine and every one of these patients went home happy.

The Day the Wharf Fell In

Prior to 1932, Mussau Islanders had fiercely resisted any contacts with Western civilisation. The situation was so dangerous that the Australian Government prohibited any contact from outsiders. A Roman Catholic priest ignored the prohibition and was promptly killed, chopped in pieces and buried.

In April, 1932, with government permission, Captain McLaren and a group of Solomon Islanders risked a similar fate and sailed to Mussau, hoping to establish a mission station. The *Veilomani* was met by angry Mussaus, armed with spears and bows and arrows. As the canoes approached the ship, the Solomon Islanders on board began to sing "Anywhere with Jesus I can Safely Go." The warriors stopped paddling and listened to the beautiful harmony. They had never heard anything like it before, and allowed Captain McLaren to go ashore and speak to their chief. Within 12 months, 170 Mussau Islanders had been converted.

With government approval, a school was opened by Pastor Atkins at Boliu on October 23, 1933.

Twenty-three years later, Colin and Melva were notified that they were to be transferred to Mussau Island where Colin was to be the superintendent of the 24-bed Boliu Hospital, principal of Boliu Central School, teaching Grades 5, 6 and 7, and District Director of Mussau, Emirau and Tench Islands. To Colin this seemed a strange decision because he was not a trained teacher yet was appointed as principal over the existing experienced national headmaster and trained teacher, Nathan Rore. Frankly, Colin was embarrassed, but Nathan Rore, who was far more qualified for the position, was humble and gave Colin his loyal support. They became great friends.

Winchee

With Pastor Les Webster in charge, the *Malalagi* was approaching Boliu, transporting Colin and Melva Winch, together with newly-born Kerry, to take up their new appointment on Mussau Island. It had been a rough crossing but as they approached Boliu and moved into quieter waters, they began to appreciate the beauty of their surroundings.

On entering Schadel Bay, Colin and Melva could see the mission station and school building, both built of native materials, on the hill to their left. To their right, they noted the principal's home and mission office, both built from permanent materials. From the wharf protruding out into deep water in the bay, they noted that paths bordered by white-washed stones had been formed leading to the school, the principal's home and mission office. The campus grass was lush and green having been trimmed with bush knives. It was a welcoming sight.

The wharf at Boliu had been constructed from bush material and needed constant repairs in the hot, humid weather. As Colin and Melva looked up to the school building, they noted that Nathan Rore, the headmaster Colin was to replace, had all the students lined up, washed and ready to welcome the new headmaster.

As the *Malalagi* approached the wharf, the students marched from the school to the wharf with Nathan Rore calling the step! "Left! Right! Left! Right!" They marched right up onto the wharf. "One! Two! Three! HALT!"

With the command to halt, all of the students stamped their feet down in unison. It was too much for the wharf timbers. There was a splintering of wood as the planks gave way and the students fell through into the water below, amid squeals of surprise and then peals of laughter.

Those on the *Malalagi* joined in the mirth but Nathan Rore was embarrassed. Climbing back on shore, the students sang a song of welcome in four-part harmony, "We're glad to welcome you to Boliu School."

Many of the students were married adults with children of their own. They were a stable influence on the younger children and made great workers in the gardens, growing food for the school and mission. Needless to say, the wharf was eventually repaired with new pylons and heavy decking timbers milled from the hard and durable Kwila trees.

The Day the Wharf Fell In

While these repairs were being carried out, Colin decided to build a horizontal bar off the side of the wharf. Bill Driscoll—one of his teachers in high school in Australia—had drilled the boys in acrobatics on a horizontal bar and this skill Colin passed on to the boys much to their enjoyment. Besides, the water below made for a soft, cool landing. It added fun to the learning process.

Boliu Central School, Mussau, students ready to sing the welcome song to the new principal and his wife. (Left) Nathan Rore, (centre) Pastor Guibau, District Director, Teacher Lausen (far right). Colin and Melva's house, top left of picture.

Lost at Sea

February 21, 1957, proved to be a special day for Colin and Melva. Kerry, their first-born daughter, was born in Rabaul about the time the family took up their new appointment.

In the tropical conditions in which they lived, infection could spread rapidly, sometimes with dire consequences. When Melva developed a severe and painful inner-ear infection, Colin decided to give her an oily penicillin injection. However, Melva developed alarming symptoms so Colin gave her a second injection, thinking the infection was rapidly worsening. This only intensified the symptoms. Melva began to ache all over, particularly in her joints until she could hardly walk. Both missionaries were alarmed.

The mission ship *Malalagi* happened to be at Boliu, so they decided that Melva should seek help from a doctor at Kavieng, New Ireland. Following prayer for safekeeping, Melva and four-month-old Kerry joined the crew on the overnight journey, leaving behind a deeply concerned husband and father whose only news was through scheduled radio contacts.

The doctor in Kavieng quickly diagnosed that Melva was allergic to penicillin and gave her an antidote, telling her she must never take penicillin again. When Colin received this news, he was greatly relieved and looked forward to his family's return. He missed both Melva and his new daughter greatly, and was sad that his action had intensified the crisis.

Four days later, the *Malalagi* was returning to Boliu, under the control of Pastor Les Webster, having collected a load of second-hand corrugated iron and steel. With him was Pastor Hugh Dickens and a national crew.

Back in Boliu, Colin knew heavy seas were running because he could hear waves pounding on the reef some distance away. Not the best sea traveller at any time, Melva became violently ill. However, this was not the major problem. The load of steel on deck was interfering with the compass, so the ship was sailing in a northeasterly direction when it

Lost at Sea

should have been heading northwest. In fact, they were many degrees too far east.

When morning came, the ship should have been at Boliu but no land was to be seen. The crew realised they were well off course and lost in heavy seas. Melva was so seasick she could not care for her baby, so Hugh Dickens kindly looked after and fed Kerry.

Not knowing their current position, the crew guessed a compass heading that they hoped would bring them to Boliu. They travelled all that day and the next night and eventually came to an atoll known as Tench Island. Had they missed this atoll, they might not have seen land for many days.

While at Tench Island, the two pastors went ashore for a few hours to meet with those living there, all of whom were Adventists. Melva chose to remain on the *Malalagi*, feeling too ill to leave her bunk. The boat at anchor in the ocean continued to roll from side to side and toss up and down, giving Melva no respite from her vomiting.

The *MV Malalagi* loading the Boliu Central School's copra bound for sale in Kavieng.

Winchee

In the meantime, Colin was almost beside himself with worry. Anger began to well up inside! What was wrong with the crew? "Lord! Please keep my dear ones and the crew safe!" he prayed.

When news finally came through that the boat was at Tench Island, Colin was confused. What were they doing at Tench Island when they should have been at Boliu several days ago? He continued with his teaching but rushed home to listen in to the morning and evening radio contacts, hoping to hear more news.

On returning to the ship, the crew set sail on a new course, which they believed would take them to Mussau. Again, the iron cargo played havoc with the compass. For two more days the *Malalagi* ploughed through rough seas before land was sighted. However, it was not Mussau but New Ireland.

The crew knew now they were not far from the town of Namatanai, so they followed the coastline northwestward until they came to Kavieng—the port from which they had departed five days previously to make the overnight trip to Boliu. Colin suggested to the crew by radio contact that they swing the ship's compass and note the deviation caused by the steel before leaving the harbour.

That evening, the *Malalagi* once more set sail for Boliu, arriving without major incident the next morning. Weakened and dehydrated by prolonged seasickness, Melva, with baby Kerry, disembarked from the boat and fell into the arms of her relieved husband. There were tears of rejoicing and prayers of thankfulness as the Winch family was reunited.

This frightening experience left Melva with a dread of ships. It had been a horrible experience for a relatively new missionary and mother.

The Queen is Drowned

While located at Boliu from 1957 to 1960, Colin was extremely busy as superintendent, school principal and District Director of Mussau, Emirau, and Tench Islands. However, in the school holidays, the family planned to hold revival meetings in the villages on Mussau Island.

Melva would gather the village children and tell stories. Toddler Kerry and baby Carol, as white kids, were a source of fascination for the dark-skinned village people. Colin borrowed a 16-millimetre projector and films such as "Faith for Today" from the Bismark–Solomons Union Mission headquarters. He also borrowed British and Australian newsreels from the government film library. Among these was a full-length feature film recording the coronation of Queen Elizabeth II. The librarian informed Colin that "The Queen is Crowned" was a valuable film and great care must be taken of it. These films made quite an impact when shown in Boliu prior to leaving on a visit to the villages on the island.

Transport was via the mission ship, the *Malalagi*, and the week-long revival meetings received a good response. The films proved popular at Lovarang as the villagers had rarely seen moving pictures before.

At the end of the series, it was time to move on to the next village. The heavy equipment was carried to a location where there was a narrow passage in the reef and Colin arranged for a huge native canoe, normally used for carrying bags of copra to the ship standing off the reef, to transport the equipment to the *Malalagi*. All of the films and the projector were wrapped in canvas to protect them from splashes of salt water as the 20 strong young men paddled the heavy canoe through the breaking waves to the mission vessel.

Winchee

The leader of the paddlers stood looking out to sea, reading the waves to determine the precise time to launch the canoe. The young paddlers, with oars in hand, lined up on each side of the canoe awaiting the command to push, then board, the canoe. Timing was critical lest the canoe be swamped.

"Push!" The command came with a degree of urgency and one lone paddler leapt into the canoe and feverishly began to paddle. The rest stood on the reef shouting instructions as the lone paddler vainly endeavoured to drive the canoe forward.

It was then Colin saw a giant swell approaching the reef. If all of the paddlers had leaped into the canoe and paddled, all would have been well, but a lone paddler had no chance against the power of the ocean. To Colin's horror, the wave crashed over the canoe and filled it with corrosive salt water from stem to stern. The films were floating in their metal containers and the projector was sloshing around within the canoe. That day, "The Queen is Crowned" became "The Queen is drowned."

Despite every effort back at Boliu to wash all the footage of every film—including "The Queen is Crowned"—with fresh water, all were ruined and a sheepish Colin sent a radiogram to Pastor John Dever, secretary of the Bismark–Solomons Union Mission, notifying him of the loss. With a great deal of apprehension, Colin awaited the reply.

Eventually it came: "Dear Colin! George Burnside recommends a blackboard and chalk as the best evangelistic aid! Greetings. John Dever."

Medical Emergencies

While living at Boliu, Colin and Melva crossed by boat to Emirau to commence a patrol. As soon as the boat arrived at the wharf, the head teacher of the Talivu mission school rushed up to Melva, notifying her that she was needed urgently at the clinic. Colin accompanied his wife but was not permitted to enter. This was "women's business"!

He gathered the family together and they joined in prayer that God would give Melva skill and ease the suffering of the poor mother. At that stage, the condition of the baby was not known, though there were grave doubts due to the prolonged labour.

On entry, Melva noted a woman lying on the concrete floor, there being no beds in the clinic. The woman was in terrible agony having been in labour for three days. Melva prayed to God for skill to bring the crisis to a successful outcome.

On examination, Melva found that the dead baby was presenting sideways and needed to be turned before the birth could be successful. For some hours, between contractions, Melva attempted to turn the baby, finally succeeding and the birth was achieved, much to the relief of the distressed mother. It was another several hours before the placenta was removed.

Melva's back ached from being on her knees, bending over the prostrate woman lying on the concrete. There was sadness that the child was stillborn but the family joined in giving thanks to God for the saving of the mother. Word spread of her treatment and Melva became greatly loved throughout Emirau.

* * *

Winchee

Back at Boliu, Colin had "men's business" to attend to. The little clinic had two wards—one for each gender. These were made of bush materials with a dispensary and storeroom made of permanent material in between. Colin dealt with surgical emergencies in this dispensary, equipped with an operating table.

One day he was called to deal with Reuben's wounds resulting from a confrontation with a huge boar. A fence had been erected around the gardens to keep out scavenging wild pigs. Reuben, a schoolboy at the time, had been patrolling the fence when he came across this pig. Armed with a sharpened piece of reinforcing rod, Reuben threw it at the pig.

The animal took offence and charged Reuben, tossing him in the air and ripping his buttocks to the bone with his tusks. He also tore the boy's scrotum.

Reuben was in pain!

It was a major wound and very dirty. Before Colin began to deal with the situation, he prayed for skill and comfort for the young man. Realising it would take a good deal of time to clean and suture, he suggested to Reuben that he give him a general anaesthetic but the patient would have none of it. He wanted to stay awake and know exactly what was going on. Despite Colin's warnings that it was going to be painful, he was adamant and told Colin to do what he had to do and forget about him.

After a heavy shot of morphine, Colin and Perere, the doctor-boy, set about cleaning the dirt from the deep wound, a task taking the best part of an hour. As a preventative to infection, US Army oily penicillin was used and 100 stitches pulled the wound together. All this time, Reuben lay quiet, periodically asking how the procedure was going.

The wound in the buttocks cared for, Colin turned his attention to the scrotum. Once cleaned, it was obvious the skin had been torn except for a minor thread. But this contained no blood vessel and so had to be snipped off. Having done what he could, Colin bowed in prayer, asking God to place His hand of healing on Reuben, a prayer that Reuben said a hearty "Amen" to!

Reuben survived, became a fine teacher and fathered numerous children. Some 15 years later, he and Colin met at Kavieng and, in

Medical Emergencies

a private showing, Reuben dropped his trousers and underwear to proudly reveal a neat scar on his buttocks.

"I was very proud of that scar," said Colin, with a wry smile.

* * *

On another occasion, Colin was called down to the dispensary at Boliu to attend to a little girl, about 10 years old, who had caught her eyelid in a cooking hook.

Each village house had a kitchen attached to the rear in which was a large box-like structure filled with earth on which they place their fires for cooking. Hanging from the ceiling would be a heavy wire shaped in the form of a hook on which they hung their cooking pots.

Apparently this girl had been playing with her brothers and ran through the kitchen, catching her eyelid on the hook. Her eyelid was almost ripped off—only hanging by a thread of skin. The father brought his injured girl to the dispensary with her eyelid hanging down her face. It was a hideous sight.

Colin examined the traumatised girl and decided that the eyelid could be saved with careful surgery. Fortunately, no damage had been done to the eyeball. Without surgery, the girl faced hideous disfigurement for the rest of her life.

After prayer to the Divine Healer for guidance and skill, the decision was made to give the girl a general anaesthetic. Before doing so, Colin asked whether she had eaten over the previous four hours. On being assured in the negative by the father, the girl was anaesthetised and Colin began the delicate task of stitching the torn eyelid back in place.

Partway through the procedure, the patient gave a big heave and stopped breathing. Rolling her on her side, Colin gave her a thump on the back. Out popped a large piece of recently eaten sweet potato and other tropical vegetables. The girl most certainly had eaten—and probably within the past hour. The obstruction removed and breathing restored, Colin completed the suturing. After a prayer of thanks to God, the little girl was returned into the care of her relieved family.

Some 12 months later, he again saw the patient and was happy with the long-term results. Apart from a slight droop of the eyelid, there was no obvious disfigurement.

Winchee

* * *

Caring for an emergency outside of the family is one thing; but an emergency within the family is a different thing altogether.

Two-year-old Kerry had been pushing baby Carol in a little pusher around the lounge-room floor of their Boliu home when she accidently upset the pusher, tipping the baby out onto the floor. Kerry fell down onto the pusher and cut her chin just below her bottom lip. Two children screamed in unison, causing Melva to run to see what was the problem. For a moment she was unsure whether to tend to the baby first or to Kerry, but the blood streaming from the cut on Kerry's chin quickly settled the issue.

An urgent message was sent for Colin to come from the school to examine the wound. Obviously it required three or four sutures and preparations were made to carry out the procedure. Melva was nursing Kerry on her knee but when the child saw the needle she resisted vigorously, fighting like a little tiger.

Kerry had experienced needles before and was having none of it!

The parents waited for her to calm down and tried again—with the same result. Eventually, they decided to just pull the wound together with sticking plaster and hope for the best. To this day, Kerry carries the scar to inform her of an incident she has no memory of.

Life on a Mission Station

Early in 1961, Colin and Melva with their two young daughters, four-year-old Kerry and two-year-old Carol, travelled to their new mission appointment at Oriomo, three hours sail up the Oriomo River from Daru and only five metres above sea level. Melva was pregnant with their third child, Nerolie, born on June 14 of that year.

En route from Port Moresby, they joined Pastor Elwyn Martin aboard the *MV Urahine*, planning to visit the mission headquarters at Karokaro on the Vailala River before going on to Oriomo. Sailing in the heavy seas of the Papuan Gulf, the boat pitched and rolled wildly. Melva and the children soon became violently seasick.

The Vailala bar was known to be extremely dangerous, particularly if a southeasterly wind was blowing—as it was on this occasion. As the boat approached the Vailala River, huge waves were crashing over the bar, sending a haze of spume heavenward. From the deck level, it was impossible to see the passage through the bar so the national captain, William, climbed up the mast in spite of the boat being tossed about like a cork, to try to guide the boat to the appropriate winding passage to the calmer deep waters of the Vailala River. It was a hazardous exercise.

The huge following swells were surfing the boat toward the bar as the brave captain strained to find the break in the pounding surf. Suddenly he shouted, "*Henia Taubada!*" ("Give it to her now, Master!")

A huge roller picked the boat up and drove it on to the sand, missing the passage. Swung side on to the pounding waves, the *Urahine* was lifted and dumped, lifted and dumped, lifted and dumped—"Boom, Boom, Boom." It was a frightening experience for all on board,

Winchee

particularly for seasick Melva as she thought of the risk to the lives of her two children.

After about half an hour of continuous pounding, the boat was pushed into the deep waters of the river. Prayers of thanks ascended and racing hearts returned to a more normal beat as the *Urahine* made its way up the river to the mission station. But it was only a temporary respite. A brief stop over and then the *Urahine* was again sailed into the open waters of the Papuan Gulf before entering the murky waters of the Oriomo River.

* * *

When the Winch family finally arrived at Oriomo, they were hit with energy-sapping intense heat and humidity. Melva's heart sank as they took occupancy of their home, a native shack constructed of Pit Pit (a type of bamboo), and beaten palm fronds woven into a wall cladding. The thatched-leaf roof was infested with rats and leaked during heavy rain.

MV Urahine tied up at the Kitomave Mission School on the Kikori River, Papuan Gulf Mission.

Life on a Mission Station

The wooden floorboards were not tongue-and-grooved and, due to shrinkage, allowed mosquitoes entry to the home. Millions of mosquitoes! They came through the windows and the walling, as well as up through the floor.

The house was elevated due to the possibility of floods, access being via a set of steps. There was no running water in the house and the smelly pit toilet was outside, some distance from the main building. Adjacent to the house was a small office on which was an iron roof that shed water into a small holding tank. This provided water for household use but involved carrying it by bucket some 100 yards (about 100 metres).

Ablutions were carried out in the privacy of darkness when the family went to the jetty, stripped to the bare necessities and tipped buckets of water over themselves. The river was crocodile-infested so they dared not swim in the cooling waters.

Mosquitoes, crocodiles and heat were not the only problems. Three types of deadly snakes were prolific in the area: the Papuan Black, the Taipan and the Death Adder. It was not unusual to find a Papuan Black curled up on the toilet seat, a frightening experience particularly at night.

One day Kerry was clambering down the steps and began to scream in terror. On the bottom step lay a deadly Taipan. With Colin frequently away, Melva had to be always on the alert.

A backwater of the Oriomo River separated the Oriomo village from the mission home. A coconut tree trunk had been felled to form a bridge across the backwater some 10 feet (3 metres) above water level. This would spring up and down as a person made the crossing.

This was a particular challenge when Melva was sometimes called out at night to deliver a village baby. Crossing the tree-trunk bridge by lantern-light was a nerve-wracking experience, with the possibility of an unwanted fall into the backwater a constant reality. Colin was often away for weeks at a time visiting the villages along the rivers, leaving Melva and the children as the only Europeans in the area. The increased responsibility of care for the children's safety sometimes meant a sleepless night of reading for the ever-alert pregnant mother.

Living conditions improved late in 1961 when David Lambert,

Winchee

a builder from Brisbane, arrived to construct a new home for the missionaries. Leaving Colin and David to this project, Melva and the girls sailed to Port Moresby to await Nerolie's birth. Again they suffered from seasickness throughout the trip.

One night, as the two men were sitting at the table eating their evening meal, Colin noticed a large Papuan Black snake dangling from the thatched ceiling directly behind David's head, while David was totally oblivious to the danger he was in.

"David. Stay still! Don't move!" said Colin.

Thinking Colin was playing a trick on him, David called out, "What do you mean?" and spun around, meeting face to face with the venomous snake.

It is arguable who got the biggest fright! Fortunately the 7-foot (2-metre) long creature dropped to the floor and slithered away.

Life in the mission field was not without excitement!

There was no relief day or night from the heat and humidity. Heavy showers would fall, followed by the blasting heat of the sun making physical work under such conditions very draining. They would cool off by taking turns for a quick dip in the cool waters of the Oriomo River while the non-swimmer would stand on the jetty watching for crocodiles. It was refreshing but a dangerous luxury!

* * *

Mail was always looked forward to but no postman made deliveries to this isolated area. To collect the mail required a day-long paddle in a canoe to Daru and a two-day return trip.

On one occasion, the two men made the journey, not using the mission launch *Diari* as this could only be used for official mission work, due to budgetary restrictions. Paddling downstream with the current was pleasurable compared with paddling against the current on the return trip. This involved an overnight stop somewhere on the bank of the Oriomo River—a risky venture due to the presence of hungry crocodiles. However, exhaustion ensured a sound sleep under a grass-roofed shelter and the crocodiles failed to take advantage of their sleeping feast.

The timber framed, fibro-clad, iron-roofed house took four months

Life on a Mission Station

to complete. Constructed on stilts to allow for any cooling breeze and to keep the rats out, the living quarters were above and the laundry and shower downstairs. This meant no more bucket showers! And no more mosquitoes at night. They were kept out by the fine-meshed screens on all windows. Melva was delighted!

* * *

The 650-mile (1050-kilometre) long Fly River is one of Papua New Guinea's longest rivers, rising in the Victor Emanuel Mountains on the Irian Jaya border and flowing through flood plains to the Gulf of Papua. In its upper course, it flows through narrow gorges, then through swampy grasslands, but by the time it reaches the sea its delta is 32 miles (53 kilometres) wide. In this delta can be seen many low-lying islands, a number of which are inhabited. The main town of the area is Daru, situated on a small island of the same name.

To reach the Fly River, Colin had to sail the *Diari II*—a 28-foot (8.5-metre) mission vessel based at Oriomo—down the Oriomo River to Daru, a trip that took a little longer than three hours. After picking up supplies, he sailed the open sea of the Papuan Gulf, heading for the north bank of the Fly River. Sailing in the Papuan Gulf with its delta waterways and 30-foot (9-metre) tides was a hazard in itself due to ever-shifting tidal mud flats. This navigational nightmare necessitated a constant watch lest the ship run aground.

The crew was made up of the national captain, Duba, and three or four volunteer crewmen who were happy to work for the pleasure of a sea-going holiday. On one such trip, Colin was at the wheel and Duba was casting the leadline into the muddy opaque water from the bow of the ship, calling the depth.

"Two fathoms, Taubada!"

"One and a half fathoms, Taubada!"

"One fathom, Taubada!"

Then Wooooom! They were firmly aground on the sand.

The crew ran from side to side, rocking the boat in unison while the captain put the engine on full throttle astern. There was no success. They were firmly held by the hard-packed sand, 90 million tons of which were washed down the Fly River every year.

Winchee

All they could do was prop the boat upright with timber props and wait six hours for the incoming tide to lift them clear. Fortunately, one of the nationals had a ball in his possession, so a hastily contrived bat enabled them to have a game of cricket on the compressed sand while they waited for nature to provide her solution.

On other expeditions on these waterways, Colin had to take precautions against being caught in a bore. A bore occurs when the leading edge of the incoming tide forms a wave—or waves—of water against the river's outgoing current. Such waves travel at increasing speed as the funnel-shaped delta narrows and can be dangerous for river shipping. It creates a roaring, rumbling sound that can be heard from a great distance. River-going boats such as the *Diari II* may surf these waves but if turned broadside may easily be capsized. When these dangers threatened, Colin would sail the *Diari II* into sheltered waters until the danger had passed, then follow in the wake of the bore.

The life of a missionary is always to expect the unexpected, a challenge that had its worries but also its excitement. Colin thrived on it!

Learning to Fly

"When once you have tasted flight, you will forever walk the earth with your eyes turned skyward, for there you have been, and there you will always long to return."—Wimmera Aero Club

While living at Boliu, Colin and Melva contacted a person in Brisbane who sent them a large package of old magazines. Among them, much to Colin's delight, were a number on aviation. While on furlough in 1958, he had been studying Greek, Hebrew, ancient history and ethics externally through London University but these magazines on aviation captured his imagination, so he switched academic pursuits to study for his Private and Commercial Pilot's licence by correspondence with Australian Civil Aviation School.

In 1961, Colin was appointed District Director of the West Papua District based in Oriomo. This huge district involved sailing the Fly River as far as the West Irian border and 10 other rivers, visiting the many villages along the banks of the waterways. It was a challenging lifestyle for all members of the family. Melva's life as a mother was made more difficult when baby Nerolie, their third daughter, periodically suffered from high fevers, causing them to question whether she may have contracted elephantiasis, a disease transmitted by mosquitoes and flies.

Despite these concerns, Colin continued with his aviation studies to the point where he was ready to sit final theory exams for both his Private and Commercial licence. It was arranged that the papers be flown from Port Moresby to Daru.

In those days, the flight was made in a Catalina (flying boat). Colin went by boat to pick them up and spoke to the captain: "My name is Winch. I understand you have some exam papers for me?"

"Yes, I do," responded the Captain, handing over the envelope containing the exams. These were duly sat under the direction of the District Commissioner.

Winchee

Two weeks later, the family were due to fly home on furlough. When the captain of the Catalina saw the name "Winch" on the passenger list, he located Colin and invited him to the flight deck once the plane was airborne. At the captain's suggestion, Colin took over the controls and flew the plane almost to Port Moresby. Regardless of the noise of the motors, Colin was both ecstatic and "hooked."

Prior to leaving on furlough, he had asked Pastor John Keith, president of the Coral Sea Union Mission, for permission to obtain his pilot's licence as a furlough assignment while in Australia. The veteran missionary replied, "Colin, the Coral Sea Union Mission will never get an aeroplane!"

* * *

On returning to Australia, Colin was not given a furlough assignment, allowing him opportunity to pursue his flying training. This he chose to do at the Wimmera Aero Club (Victoria) under the tuition of Dick Hunt. This club had been established in 1947 and undertook training at Nhill, Horsham (Melva's home town), Warracknabeal, Hamilton and Birchip.

The Wimmera Aero Club's Cessna 172 in which Colin commenced his flying training in 1962.

Learning to Fly

To obtain a Private Licence took 40 hours of flying and 165 hours for a Commercial Licence at the cost of 5 pounds 10 shillings per hour—a lot of money in those days. Colin was fortunate, however, because Dick Hunt offered the cash-strapped missionary the opportunity to fly him to his various other flying schools at a cost of two pounds per hour, a major saving and an opportunity to accumulate flying hours at a rapid rate.

Even more hours of flying were accumulated when a farmer, George Smith, offered Colin the use of his Tiger Moth for the cost of fuel and oil. This was a Godsend and the smiling missionary availed himself of many hours of circuit training and aerobatics out of what is now known as the "George Smith Memorial Airstrip" at Birchip.

In the meantime, no solution had been found to Nerolie's worrying health issue. Every six weeks, the fevers would return with high temperatures and questions arose as to the wisdom of returning to the mission field. When the Wimmera Aero Club board offered Colin a fulltime job as an instructor, after discussions with Melva, Colin decided to accept the position and notified Pastor Laurie Naden, Division secretary, that they would not be returning to the mission field.

But two weeks later—on a Sabbath afternoon—Colin and family were seated in their Morris Minor at the end of an airstrip and became conscience-smitten. They must return to the mission field!

To Dick Hunt's great disappointment but the church's satisfaction, Colin notified Pastor Naden of the decision but requested that due to Nerolie's medical issues they be transferred away from Oriomo. Colin was appointed as District Director to Maprik in the Sepik District, a mission station at the elevation of 800 feet (240 metres). Mosquitoes were less of a problem at this elevation. However, Melva remained in the homeland for three months while solutions were sought for Nerolie's medical issues.

* * *

On returning to Papua New Guinea in 1963, Colin took up his appointment at Maprik and endeavoured to further his experience as a pilot by offering to fly for the Mission Aviation Fellowship on his days off. This offer was declined but gladly accepted by the Catholic Church, who were flying a Cessna 180 when Colin approached them.

Winchee

Needing to gain flying experience in Papua New Guinea, Colin applied to the Coral Sea Union Mission to fly for Stolair—a small charter airline in Central and Western Papua based in Port Moresby—during his holiday time and was given permission to do so. This proved valuable as it gave him experience in flying in New Guinea's uniquely dangerous conditions.

About this time, Colin became aware that a fellow missionary, Len Barnard, held a Private Licence and was keen to use planes in the mission work of the church. Both men had spent days tramping muddy leech-infested swamps, fording rushing streams, labouring up sheer mountain sides, and cutting their way through tropical jungle, while above them planes were covering distances in minutes that took them days on foot.

At that stage, the two missionaries had not met but Colin wrote to Len, saying, "I've got a Commercial Licence; you've got a Private Licence. Let's buy a plane between us and share it in our work here in the mission field!"

Largely due to Len Barnard's ability to solicit funds, enough money was raised to buy a new Cessna 180. Action was passed by the appropriate church authorities for the use of the plane in mission work in New Guinea.

* * *

While serving at Maprik, Colin and Melva met Kwesekien, a crippled but faithful member of the Maprik Sabbath school. Every Sabbath, in sunshine or rain, this 10-year-old girl would leave her home around 7 am and crawl for two hours over rough pathways, crossing two mountain streams in order to be at Sabbath school on time. She was never known to be late.

Her smiling face revealed her enjoyment of hearing the King's Heralds singing as recorded on a LP record. She happily joined in singing choruses, loved listening to stories and was particularly intrigued by the colourful pictures on the picture roll.

Colin wrote up her story, which was printed on the front page of the *Review and Herald* of April 9, 1964. This drew a generous financial response from church members around the world and a suggestion that

Kwesekien be taken to Sopas Hospital for assessment and treatment by Dr Yeatts.

With the plane now a reality, Colin had the privilege of flying her and her father from Maprik to Wabag. Having never been in an aeroplane, she clung to him in terror. The father joined the flight, not so much out of care for his daughter but for the kudos of flying.

Such flights fulfilled the dream of two far-sighted missionaries. No longer did they "walk the earth with their eyes turned skyward" but spent happy hours of mission service on land and sea—and in the skies!

Candidate for the *Kalabus*

Protein was often lacking in the diet of the indigenous inhabitants of the mountainous backbone of New Guinea. Pigs and bush rats provided the main source, but human flesh was also seen as a culturally acceptable before Westerners arrived to bring about change. Government officials sought to enforce legislation against cannibalism; missionaries preached the gospel of "Love one another" or "Love your enemies, don't eat them!"

There were no cemeteries in Kukukuku country. Apart from caves high up on the mountains where the smoked remains of village chiefs are propped overlooking their villages, burial was not practised. Fierce warriors and skilled hunters, these short, stocky inhabitants from the remote Kukukuku mountain regions were feared by other nationals throughout Papua New Guinea. Asking a national carrier to enter Kukukuku territory was akin to asking him to sign his own death warrant. Fear would show itself by trembling and other physical manifestations.

It was believed that to eat the flesh of an enemy, either captured or killed in battle, was to inherit the skill and bravery of the victim. It was preferable to capture and fatten for food rather than kill and risk having less flesh to consume. Consequently many victims were simply taken by ambush, had their knees broken so they were unable to escape, fattened, then eaten. In other areas, relatives who died were cooked and eaten.

In 1967, while living in Kainantu, Colin engaged in a 16-day patrol into Kukukuku territory, taking the gospel story to clusters of villages perched on the mountainsides and in the valleys. He took with him

Candidate for the *Kalabus*

his District Director pastor and flew to Wonenara where he received permission from the Kiup (Patrol Officer) to tie the mission plane down in the parking bay of the airstrip in his absence and also notified the Kiup of his proposed itinerary. Paid in salt, carriers and a *tanimtok* (translator) from the Adventist village were employed and the group tramped for the 16 days in mountains and high mountain valleys at altitudes of between 4000 and 9000 feet (1200 and 2700 metres).

It was on one of these days that the translator informed him that the next village had been a cannibal village in times past. They had a deep pit in which they had placed their captives while they fattened them in preparation for killing for a ritual feast.

While Colin was well aware of these past practices and knew from personal observation the Kukukuku's skills with bow and arrow, he had no fear for his personal safety. He knew the villagers would never kill and eat a white man, even if it was only out of fear for the consequences.

As much as possible, the villages were notified in advance of the proposed visit. Sometimes it was through a resident native missionary. Other times, a message written in Pidgin was thrown from the mission plane and fluttering to the ground, attracted the attention of one of the village residents. Contact was made with each village chief on arrival and, after receiving permission, picture rolls were brought out and gospel stories were told.

Whether speaking to Westerners or nationals, Colin was a great storyteller and would soon have everyone's attention. He found that when a Kukukuku national was won to the gospel, he or she often showed great shame and remorse for their cannibalistic past.

* * *

In 1962, Colin Winch met Ron Firns in New Guinea, the managing director of Stolair, who offered him a job. Colin informed him he was a missionary but indicated interest in gaining flying experience during his holidays. When holiday time came in 1963, Colin was given permission by church leaders to gain experience in flying for the charter airline on a voluntary basis. Ron was delighted to have such an enthusiastic and qualified pilot, particularly as it was not going to cost wages.

He based Colin at Daru with a Cessna 180—the type of plane the

Winchee

church would first use in Papua New Guinea the next year. During that holiday time, Colin flew all over the western districts of Papua.

One day, Colin was asked to fly to the Nomad River government patrol post on a charter pick-up. The Nomad River area was known as the last stronghold of cannibalism and for that reason the government had placed restrictions on Caucasians entering the area because it was deemed too dangerous.

On arrival, Colin found he was to provide transport for a national police officer and a handcuffed prisoner who was to be jailed for eating his deceased grandmother. The poor man was terrified as he was placed in the plane. Some of his tribesmen had been "eaten" by the white man's bird and had never been seen again. He was sure he was about to die and be eaten.

As the plane taxied to the end of the airstrip in preparation for takeoff, he hung his head between his knees and cupped his hands

Nomad River cannibals in the Western District of Papua soberly pose for a photo.

Candidate for the *Kalabus*

above his head, his whole body shaking in terror. The motor roared into life and the plane gathered speed along the runway, then lifted into the air. Below could be seen the green canopy of the thick Papuan jungle and a network of waterways snaking their way to the sea.

Both Colin and the kindly police officer encouraged the terrified prisoner to lift his head and view the scenery below. But the poor terrified man would have none of it. He was going to die! There was no doubt!

After the two-hour flight to Daru, the plane landed and the prisoner was taken to the *kalabus* (prison) where he would remain until he was considered "civilised" enough to return to his own village.

In the meantime, Colin took off for another flight that would gain him experience for the longed-for day when he would be flying over the same terrain in the work of the gospel.

Establishing New Airstrips

Kombot is a small village about 2000 feet (600 metres) above sea level in the Prince Alexander Mountains. In church parlance, it is in the Maprik district of the Sepik Mission. A small school caring for Kindergarten- to Grade Two-level children under the care of national teachers had been established there, so it was of interest to Colin while he was the District Director located at Maprik. On a number of occasions, he hiked into the school while on patrol.

As the Cessna 180 *Andrew Stewart* had arrived in Papua New Guinea and was shared between Len Barnard and himself, Colin was ever on the lookout for suitable sites on which to form an airstrip. He noted the school playground and, with his eyes, followed an extension of the ridge, thinking all the time that it could be made into a short but serviceable airstrip.

He revealed his thoughts to the headmaster of the school and together they walked up the steep ridge to further ascertain the possibilities. Certainly the ridge was rugged and steep but it was agreed there was a definite possibility, provided the Luluai (government-appointed village chief) and Tultul (government-appointed subordinate) would give their support to the project. It would require much hard labour using mattocks, shovels, rakes and other hand tools. Rocks, excess soil and unwanted debris would be carted away in native baskets.

Flying the *Andrew Stewart*, Colin made a number of slow, low flights over the school's playing field from north to south, dropping mattocks, shovels, rakes and other hand-held equipment so that clearing the land could proceed. He was assisted by Pastor Reggie, a Solomon Island worker, who discharged the tools through the open doorway of the

Establishing New Airstrips

plane. Welfare bags were also dropped as tokens of appreciation of the hard work being done.

Colin had emphasised the necessity of a smooth landing strip but his idea of smooth and that of the local people was very different. They were familiar with seeing vehicles negotiating the rough mountain roads and, to them, a plane was like a car that flies. The finished landing strip consequently was not only short—at a little short of 1000 feet (300 metres)—but resulted in a shuddering stop as the small wheels coped with the many surface variations.

Any pilot planning to land on the Kombot strip needed to do low-flying checks due to soil erosion after heavy rain. Colin had an arrangement with the local mission worker to stand in the middle of the landing strip with arms raised above his head if the site was deemed safe for a landing. If the worker's hands were waving in a criss-cross fashion at knee level, Colin knew not to attempt a landing.

The first landing, south to north up the steep slope, took place on December 13, 1966, in the presence of a large gathering of excited

A crowd of local people greet the landing of the first plane at Kombot.

Winchee

nationals. Colin subsequently made many landings at Kombot, but it was not an airstrip used by other mission pilots due to its length and steepness.

* * *

Papua New Guinea is a land of contrasts with towering mountains shedding daily rainfall into a multitude of streams that, in turn, flow into major river systems. The Nagum River flows into the mighty Sepik River—one of the largest rivers in the country.

On the banks of the Nagum River is the Nagum Central School, one of the most isolated schools in the Coral Sea Union Mission (now known as the Papua New Guinea Union Mission). It was the senior school in the Sepik Mission.

Max Miller, with his wife Val, had been the first principal, to be replaced three years later by Alwyn Campbell and his wife Edna. Alwyn was no stranger to mission service, being the son of veteran missionary Alexander John Campbell.

To travel to Wewak by road from the school in case of emergency would mean a journey of up to 11 hours over hazardous, rough and boggy roads. In a boarding school of 200 pupils living in a clearing in a tropical jungle, medical emergencies were not infrequent.

Living at Maprik from 1963 to 1966, the Winch family were the nearest European neighbours to the Campbells. In the light of the planned arrival of the Cessna 180, Colin and Alwyn discussed the desirability for a landing strip at the school, the nearest one being owned by the Catholic mission almost 4 miles (6 kilometres) away. The distance does not sound great but the link was by a very poor road and the necessity to cross the Nagum River, often subject to flooding.

Clearing of the land for the desired landing strip was to prove a major enterprise spread over five years. A prolonged negotiation with local people was necessary to obtain permission to cut down bush along the approach area across the Nagum River. Students spent their mornings in the classroom and their afternoons at work, either in the school gardens or clearing the jungle. Massive Kwila hardwood trees dug their roots into the rich alluvial soil. Two chainsaws were purchased and these roared into life in the afternoons, felling the giants of the jungle. A half

Establishing New Airstrips

dozen good-quality axes also were put to good use by male students aged between 15 and 19. It was a gigantic undertaking and a slow battle.

Builder Merv Polley had set up a mill at the school and the David Brown tractor was used to drag the logs to the mill where they were turned into timber for staff houses. There was an excess of logs and these were dragged into heaps and set alight. Kwila trees burned beautifully, the fires even devouring the underground roots. It seemed a waste to burn such valuable timber but there was no alternative if the airstrip was to become a reality.

Brian Faull replaced Alwyn as headmaster before the strip was ready for landing. Late in 1967, Colin tested the surface by driving the school Land Rover at speed up and down the strip and concluded it was suitable for landing.

Brian drove Colin to the Catholic airstrip to pick up the mission plane and together they stood beside the aeroplane and prayed for God's blessing on the landing attempt.

Colin took off and was in the Nagum circuit area in two minutes. After several test runs, DCA Control was advised and, with a prayer in his heart, Colin commenced the approach. The plane descended into the approach path with the tall forest towering above as he sped down this leafy corridor. Two coconut palms flicked past close to the wheels and then the river sped underneath and some children could be seen playing in its cool clear waters.

As Colin passed over the high river embankment, he noticed Pastor Richter—the church's director of education—and the students of the school lining both sides of the aerodrome, all of whom were hoping and praying for a successful landing. The principal's house flashed past on the right, the headmaster's house on the left. The wheels thundered and rattled on the rough turf-and-gravel strip, and the tiny tail wheel bounced madly on the rough surface.

It was July 28, 1967. Colin had landed safely, and he praised God for another mission station rescued from isolation by Adventist aviation.

Nagum became the first school in the Australasian Division to have its own landing strip and medical emergencies could now be handled quickly.

Winchee

* * *

The establishment of an airstrip at Karaisa at the head of the Agaiambo Swamp some 45 miles (75 kilometres) southeast of Popondetta is a different story. Karaisa is also the site of a district school and the district headquarters of the North East Papuan Mission.

Before Adventist mission aviation, access was only by boat, the swamp area being famous for mud, mosquitoes and ferocious crocodiles. The five-hour trip from Oro Bay, near Popondetta, to the mouth of the Yupuru River was followed by a two-hour trip up the river to Karaisa, a major undertaking and time-waster in light of the later 20-minute flight from Popondetta to Karaisa.

In August, 1968, Colin was invited to be a delegate and speaker at Karaisa, making the initial visit by boat. The day after his arrival, he took a walk behind the church and noted a large playing field clear of the swamp. Seeing with a pilot's eye, he discerned the area could be extended a little at each end of the playground, thus becoming suitable for a short landing strip. All that needed to be done was to cut down the Kunai grass and level a couple of humps.

He approached the president of the mission, asking, "How would you like to have a landing strip here at Karaisa?"

The question met with an enthusiastic response, not only from the president, but also from the local people present at the meetings. By the time the meetings ended, the cleared land was ready for an inaugural landing on the 900-foot (270-metre) strip.

Colin proposed to return to Oro Bay by mission boat and return from Popondetta next day to make the landing. Before taking his leave, he asked the teacher to make a small fire so the smoke would indicate the wind direction.

On returning in the plane with the president in the passenger seat, Colin noted that instead of a small fire, in their enthusiasm, the locals had lit a large fire of Kunai grass. Huge billows of smoke were obliterating the approach to the landing strip so Colin had to carry out a number of low-flying passes in order to clear the air sufficiently to make the landing.

Without more ado, he set up the approach and successfully landed the Cessna. Immediately, the plane was surrounded by the excited

Establishing New Airstrips

delegates. As Colin and the president alighted they were picked up and triumphantly paraded on the shoulders of strong nationals, with an entourage of joyful followers.

Selected dignitaries were taken on a short flight to celebrate the opening of yet another time-saving airstrip for the church. God was blessing His work, which went forward in leaps and bounds, significantly due to the aviation ministry.

* * *

It would be an understatement to say that Atoifi Adventist Hospital, located on the shores of the Uru Harbour on the eastern side of Malaita, Solomon Islands, has had a colourful history. Three Australian missionaries have lost their lives there. Brian Dunn and Lance Gersbach were murdered and Lens Larwood died as a result of a tractor accident.

The hospital grew over time as funds became available. It was

A new airstrip is born at Karaisa village, East Papua Mission. This airstrip was cleared and ready for landing in three days when the pilot challenged the visiting delegates on the first day of meetings.

Winchee

established in 1963 as a service to the remote Uru Harbour region and with the intent of training nurses who would give service throughout Melanesia. Until a landing strip was built, the hospital could only be reached by sea.

In his position as Union Youth and Health Director as well as Mission Pilot, Colin visited Atoifi and in discussion with Lens Larwood, ascertained the possibility of building an airstrip adjacent to the hospital. Colin was extremely doubtful that the heavily-timbered, semi-swamp could be turned into an airstrip but the hard-working, put-his-hand-to-anything Lens was certain it could be done and set out to prove it, despite the land having two creeks running through it.

Two visiting Sydney Adventist Hospital nurses—Cheryl Borgas and Dawn Maberly—had caught a vision for an airstrip at the Atoifi Hospital and set about raising funds for the project on returning to Australia. The onsite work began in August, 1973, with diverting the creeks and

Atoifi Hospital director Lens Larwood and his men cleared thick jungle and diverted a stream to build an airstrip for the nearby hospital on Uru Harbour on the northeast coast of Malaita, Solomon Islands.

Establishing New Airstrips

draining the swamp. Two large draining channels, one on each side of the proposed landing strip, were dug to carry away the water. The mission tractor possibly spent more time bogged than actually clearing, even though it was fitted with dual wheels. Atoifi is renowned for its rainfall. It is either raining or going to rain and this hindered the progress of the work.

Giant trees had to be removed and when Gordon Lee saw the methods being used, he suggested to Lens that the trees be blasted out with gelignite. He showed Lens how to go about it and this proved very effective.

A problem occurred when Lens rushed back into the area immediately the smoke cleared, not realising this would result in severe headaches. Pastor Lee informed him not to enter the area again until 24 hours after the blasts.

The felled trees were cut up and, when suitably round and straight, used as rollers to level the surface. There was a danger when towed down the slope for the log to keep rolling, even though the towing tractor had stopped! Gravel was carted from a nearby river by tractor and trailer and rolled into the soft earth, giving firmness necessary for planes to land safely.

Lens put his heart and soul into completing the airstrip, while still carrying out his other duties at the hospital. He did an incredible job being so personally involved in more than 6500 man hours that the airstrip took to be ready for operation.

On December 2, 1975, after delays due to unfavourable weather, Colin Winch made the first landing. Two hundred people watched as the Aztec did a low inspection flight before swinging around and touching down. It was a happy and historic occasion. Following a dedicatory prayer, some of the local owners of the land were given a joy ride, much to their delight.

* * *

These four new airstrips were typical of the 10 new landing strips in which Colin Winch was directly involved. His burning desire was to facilitate the spread of the gospel. He regularly gave thanks to God for men like Alwyn Campbell and Lens Larwood who shared his dream.

Another Perspective:

There was one reason that particularly encouraged the use of mission planes for transporting our national workers who were due for furloughs. Commercial boats were designed for the transport of cargo—mainly copra—and had no accommodation arrangements for passengers. These had to sleep on deck. Such boats often called at many ports to deliver cargo and mail, making the journey unduly long and difficult, particularly for mission staff, and even more impractical for single females.

On one occasion, transporting three families from the Solomon Islands to New Guinea, it was decided to put these passengers on the *MV Polurrian* as there was no plane to get them to Rabaul faster than this boat. The families boarded the ship as it finished loading copra at Numa and headed up the east coast of Bougainville to Sohano, arriving there with crew and more than 80 passengers aboard on Thursday afternoon, March 28, 1963.

From information available later, it was found that the ship sailed from Sohano into the rough waters of the open sea and at 10 pm capsized, giving no warning and no time to send out distress messages. The Adventists on board were Hoke, his wife and one young daughter; Moffat, his wife and two young children; Daniel Viva, his wife Jean and two children; and Bill who was returning home to Rabaul after making tanks in Bougainville. These families were all friends who were awakened from sleep as the boat began to roll over.

Without success, Hoke tried to get a lifebelt before jumping into the water. His wife and small daughter were trapped under the boat as it capsized and, although his wife surfaced, their daughter was never seen again.

Moffat and his family jumped into the water and two life jackets were thrown to them. Daniel and family were able to get into the water with life jackets and were fortunate to scramble onto a life raft.

Later Hoke and his wife shared a life raft with Moffat and his family. These three families aboard two life rafts were separated in the darkness by the winds and rough seas.

Establishing New Airstrips

The next day—Friday—a third raft, with the chief engineer and some other crew members aboard, joined the raft on which the families of Hoke and Moffat were survivors.

Sadly, on Sabbath one of the children was seen to die from exposure but, after much heartfelt prayer and to the joy of all aboard, revived. That night Hoke and Moffat saw a bright light and an angel standing on an island. They took it as an omen they would be saved. They were picked up by a rescue boat about 4.30 the next afternoon (Sunday).

Daniel, Jean and their two children had felt secure on their raft. However, on Friday afternoon, they were joined by several crew members, crowding the raft. On Sabbath, they were pushed off the raft and given driftwood to cling to. Fortunately they still had the two life jackets but later that sad Sabbath, the two children died from exposure.

During the night, a small shark or fish attacked Daniel and started tearing at his leg, eating the flesh. Although Daniel urged her to protect herself by swimming away from him, Jean initially refused and tried to hold his head above water while the attacker was endeavouring to pull him under. Finally, she had to swim away and leave her beloved husband to his horrific fate.

During Sunday, Jean noticed the raft from which she and her family had been ejected. She swam toward it but was refused climbing aboard. They did give her permission to hold on to the rope around the edge of the raft. Later that day, after watching her children die and seeing her husband eaten by fish, she was rescued, having spent 30 hours of the 67 hours since the *Polurrian* capsized, swimming in the rough seas.

Bill, the church member on return from Bougainville to Rabaul, managed to cling to a floating 44-gallon drum and was also rescued and delivered to Rabaul by the *MV Slitan*, which carried all of the rest of the 28 survivors—21 of whom were crew members, the rest being Seventh-day Adventist passengers.

Boating tragedies such as these resulted in mission plane travel being seen as a God-send. It prevented many heartaches and hastened the work of the gospel.

—*Eddie Piez, retired church administrator*

The Drop

Sumumuni was a small village of approximately 100 people in the Western Sepik, approximately 20 miles (32 kilometres) from the West Irian border. Situated on flat land alongside a rushing mountain stream adjacent to bush-clad mountains, it had been recently opened to the Adventist Church. A small school with a national teacher in charge had been established.

Colin was familiar with Sumumuni, having spent two days hiking into it on a previous occasion. He knew it did not have an airstrip, but had noted a school playing field. As welfare supplies became available, these were flown out by plane and dropped to the various villages. One of these airdrops was scheduled for the Sumumuni playing field. The teacher was alerted of the date and asked to notify all the village inhabitants to stay indoors to avoid the risk of getting hurt by the 65-pound (30-kilogram) bags dropping from the sky.

Pastor Elwyn Raethel, Sepik Mission president, demonstrates how the bags of clothing are dropped when Pilot Colin gives the signal.

The Drop

The door on the passenger side of the plane was removed and mission president Elwyn Raethel was strapped into the "ventilated" seat. Colin gave careful instructions as to procedure. Each bag was to be ejected from the plane at the precise moment he said "Drop." Recipient village names were written on the bags, which were then stored for easy access in the rear of the passenger's seat. On this occasion, Sumumuni was to receive three of these bags containing clothing and bars of Sunlight soap.

"Lord! Today we fly to the villages to drop these bags of clothing," they prayed before taking off. "Please may Your protecting hand be on us as we fly, and bring us safely home again, we pray!"

Shortly after takeoff, Colin was circling the playing field at Sumumuni, throttling the engine to let the villagers know the Adventist plane had arrived. He took note of the ground surface, checked the wind direction and velocity, and determined when he came opposite an outdoor toilet building he would call for the drop.

The new Sumumuni Airstrip situated close to the
West Irian border in the West Sepik District.

Winchee

As Colin flew the plane toward the designated spot, losing altitude until he was only a few feet above ground level, Elwyn reached for the first bag labelled "Sumumuni" and positioned it at the door opening.

"Drop," called Colin and the bag of clothing and soap went tumbling to the ground. Bouncing a couple more times, it cartwheeled across the surface of the playing field in the slipstream of the plane.

Colin gave the plane full throttle and climbed skyward in preparation for the next drop. A local teenage boy who had been under the school building dashed out, picked up the bag and ran back with it to the school.

Colin began his approach once more, wing flaps down to slow the plane. "Drop"—and the second bag spiralled earthward. Again the young man ran out to retrieve the bag. Dressed only in a pair of shorts, his ebony skin glistened in the sunlight and his well-formed muscles rippled as he effortlessly lifted the bag and delivered it to the teacher's house.

Female students had been watching through the school windows. Seeking to impress, the young warrior looked up and said, "*Yupela meri yu lukluk gut, bai mi kesim dispela beg!*" ("You girls watch now. I'm going to catch this bag!")

Impressed, with the traditional shake of the hand, they replied, "*Yu wanpela men tru!*" ("You are truly a brave man!")

Colin knew nothing of this and on the third approach flew a little higher. On each approach, he had been flying at high nose altitude, meaning the plane's nose was elevated, obscuring his vision of point of impact as the bags hit the ground. However, as he tilted the plane to make it easier for the bag to be pushed from the open door, Elwyn observed that the young man had run onto the playing field and was positioning himself directly under the flight path of the plane. There he stood with outstretched arms waiting to catch the bag.

"Drop!" The bag hurtled earthward, straight onto the chest of the warrior. Crashing to the ground, he was somersaulted backward in the wake of the plane, still clutching the bag. There he lay, spread-eagled and not moving. The girls, together with their teacher, ran out and surrounded him. "*Oi yu wanpela men tru!*" ("You are truly a brave man!")

The young warrior did not move. Nor did he respond. He was unconscious.

Someone ran for a bucket and, dipping it in the river, filled it with water and doused the wounded warrior's face. Slowly he regained consciousness and with blurred vision noted the ring of anxious eyes looking down at him. As his wits returned he exclaimed, "*Nau mi savi tru! Bihain mi no ken wokim dispela kain samting!*" ("I have learned my lesson. I will never try that again!")

Given the details of the story on a later visit to the village, Elwyn chuckled over the incident until the day of his death.

The simplest way to deliver welfare clothing bags to isolated villages in Papua New Guinea. Notice the right-hand door has been removed to allow accurate dropping.

A Tragic Death

Keith Ballard and Marilyn Hardy met at Avondale College in 1961. Keith was studying to be a minister and Marilyn a secretary. Friendship developed into romance when Marilyn decided to train to be a nurse at the Sydney Sanitarium and Hospital. Keith was highly respected at college being Assistant Dean of Men in his last two years of study, as well as president of the Ministerial League.

On graduating in 1963, he was appointed to the South Australian Conference to work with Pastor John Coltheart in an evangelistic campaign in Adelaide. Keith enjoyed his evangelistic work and in his second year cared for churches in the Upper Murray, as well as conducting an evangelistic campaign in Waikerie, the "Citrus Capital of South Australia."

January 17, 1966, proved a happy day for Keith and Marilyn as they were united in marriage by Pastor Clive Barritt in the Nunawading Church (Victoria). The newlyweds gave team-ministry to their pastoral responsibilities in South Australia and had given no thought to overseas mission service.

Missionaries with a minister–nurse combination were highly sought after at that time but it still came as a surprise when their president, Pastor Les Coombe, notified them of a call to mission service in Papua New Guinea, replacing Colin and Melva Winch at Maprik. The young couple had only been married 12 months and were successful in their work in the Upper Murray, but having prayed about the call, and believing all calls were from God, they looked forward to the new challenge with excitement.

Keith and Marilyn wrote to Colin and Melva seeking information about the language, culture and needs of this new country. Colin advised them to freight in advance by ship personal belongings, food supplies and tools useful in mission service in the hope that these would be waiting on their arrival.

Keith and Marilyn flew to Wewak in January, 1967 to find that their

A Tragic Death

freight had not arrived, so they lodged temporarily in a transit house on the Sepik Mission compound. Marilyn busied herself learning Pidgin English, while Keith worked with Pastor Les Parkinson, president of the Sepik Mission, visiting outlying mission posts.

While on one of these visits, it had been raining heavily turning the road surface into a quagmire. The Land Rover in which Les and Keith were travelling became bogged. As they worked to free it, Keith staked his foot on a twig and noticed an immediate pain.

On arrival home, he complained to Marilyn of his injury. She examined his foot but could see no visible wound. Thinking he had a low tolerance to pain, she bathed the foot with an antiseptic solution.

Overnight the foot swelled up and became red. Keith was taken to the Wewak hospital and given antibiotics. Repeated visits were made to the hospital as the infection worsened until finally Keith was admitted, then transferred by commercial flight to the larger hospital at Lae.

Pastor Parkinson spoke to the medical staff urging that Keith be airlifted to the Sydney Sanitarium and Hospital but was assured they had everything under control. It was not to be. Keith's condition worsened dramatically and he became delirious and died.

Heartbroken after only a few months of marriage, Marilyn faced burying her beloved husband in a strange land and returning to Australia alone. All their dreams of a lifetime of mission service were crushed in the mud.

The cemetery was located at the end of the airstrip. As Pastors Parkinson, McCutcheon and Mave led out in the solemn service the peace was shattered by the roar of DC3 aeroplane and other light planes taking off over the heads of the many mourners.

It was a bitter experience, not only for Marilyn but, as the news spread throughout the various mission outposts, for other missionaries, it was a stark reminder of how virulent tropical infections can be.

After the funeral, Coral Sea Union Mission president Pastor McCutcheon asked Colin to fly Marilyn to Maprik as she wished to see the spot where she and Keith were to have worked. On a glorious morning several days later, the *Malcolm Abbott* took off from the Lae airstrip with Colin at the controls and Marilyn in the co-pilot's seat. As they became airborne, the fresh soil and flowers on Keith's grave were

Winchee

clearly visible. How Marilyn's heart must have ached—and Colin had difficulty seeing the plane's instruments because of the tears welling up in his eyes.

The weather was gloriously fine for the two-and-a-half hour flight to Maprik. It seemed as if God was beaming special love on Marilyn as the beauties of the landscape unfolded below them. There was the mighty Markham River emptying its load of silt into the Huon Gulf. They flew through a pass between towering mountains, normally covered in cloud but on this day standing out in sharp relief against a cobalt sky. It was these bush-clad 13,000-foot (4000-metre) mountains that gave Papua New Guinea the reputation of being a perilous place to fly. Then appeared the Ramu River, which flowed in the opposite direction to the Markham. As the Ramu Valley gradually widened, the distant blue waters of Astralabe Bay could be seen, together with the buildings of Madang, glittering in the sunshine. Colin had never flown on such a clear New Guinean day.

On arrival at Maprik, they circled the mission station a number of times giving Marilyn an aerial view of the beautiful cottage that would

Colin and Melva's home base at Maprik in the Sepik Mission.
The home was built by former resident Pastor Syd Stocken.

A Tragic Death

have been her home. Then they landed on a nearby grass airstrip. The walk to the mission station was via a cool mountain stream and took about 15 minutes. On arrival, the local staff gave a warm but subdued welcome, showing sympathy for Marilyn's loss. During the 30 minutes spent on tour of the complex, Marilyn carried herself with poise and dignity.

But what suffering was experienced behind that brave exterior. Colin was also sorrowing. Prior to their recent transfer to Kainantu, he and his family had spent four happy years at Maprik and he was distressed that Keith and Marilyn could not experience the same joy.

On the return journey, Colin landed the plane at Wewak to refuel and pick up some of Marilyn's possessions for her return flight to Australia. Ironically, she observed a ship on the horizon, which proved to be the one bringing their personal effects loaded in Australia five months previously.

After returning Marilyn to the loving care of Dulcie McCutcheon, Colin flew home to Kainantu. As a warm welcome was extended to him, the pent up emotions of the day broke loose and he burst into tears. It all seemed so pointless, so unfair.

"It was while we were sitting down to dinner that it happened," Colin recalled. "The flood gates opened. I wept and could not stop. Melva understood. She put her arms around me, gave me a kiss on the back of my head and gathered the children into another room. I mourned alone."

Another Perspective:

Colin was one of the pilots flying for the church when I was headmaster of our Nagum school, 40 miles (65 kilometres) south of Wewak. Occasionally, he would fly over the school to say "hello" by working the throttle and dipping the wings. Sometimes he would deliver an "express delivery message" by throwing out the window a note wrapped around a pebble. We certainly didn't mind the interruption to our regular classroom activities, as there would be a sudden mass exodus, accompanied by much excitement and yelling. We all loved our mission plane.

On one occasion, Colin and his family paid us a visit in the bush at Nagum. In our large school gardens, we happened to have a good supply of beautiful sweet corn ready to be harvested. Edna cooked a goodly supply of delicious corn cobs and served them up on a large dish on the dining room table, together with other good food.

Our good pilot-friend took a liking to this delicacy and really made himself at home. In order to cover up his over-indulgence, he surreptitiously slipped two empty corncobs on to his neighbour's empty plate in order to give the impression of he, Colin, being a self-controlled gentleman. He did have a wicked sense of humour!

—*Alwyn Campbell, missionary educator*

To Go or Not To Go

When expatriate missionaries from the Pacific islands get together to share memories, the conversation may sometimes include toilet stories. Living in the homeland with modern flush conveniences, one might have little comprehension of the primitive facilities—and sometimes total lack of facilities—that existed in the mission field.

Expatriate missionaries from Western backgrounds tend to be private in certain aspects of daily functions. They like to shower privately, dress privately, and eliminate body wastes in private. This may create problems in remote mission outposts, and sometimes in not-so-remote locations as well. One faces a major adjustment in values or put up with great discomfort as one resists the call of nature in the presence of curious onlookers.

Children of any ethnic background are inquisitive creatures and those living in the islands of the South Pacific are no exception. When faced with adults of a different race, colour and style of dress, natural curiosity is intensified. Questions race through their young minds: "What do they eat? Why do they dress differently to us? What do they look like when they don't wear those clothes? Do they go to the toilet the same as we do?"

Colin recalls a toilet on an island in the Gilbert Islands. The building itself had been built on stilts out in the lagoon and was reached by a long, slender coconut palm, which had been felled and reached from the shore to the toilet. As one cautiously made one's way along the palm, endeavouring not to fall into the lagoon, the palm began to bounce rhythmically, causing the toilet building to rock backwards and forwards. If one needed urgent relief, the crossing became all the more hazardous. At least it was a successful warning device to anyone seated in the toilet!

On arrival in the toilet building, one could have the choice of five holes cut through a long plank suspended above the lagoon. It was a family-sized toilet and frequently so used.

Winchee

The embarrassment came when Colin noted that all the children in the village became aware that an event of some significance was about to take place. They sat on the beach awaiting the inevitable as he cautiously but very publicly made his way across the felled coconut palm to the very conspicuous "out-house." In spite of calls from the parents to come away, the children remained to satisfy their curiosity as to whether the white man went to the toilet just like them.

No wonder expatriates tended to wait until darkness to make the hazardous journey to answer nature's call. But to do so increased the risk of an unexpected dip in the lagoon because the crossing of the palm-trunk bridge with a lantern in one hand and a toilet roll in the other was even more hazardous than in daytime.

* * *

During the time the Winch family was at Boliu, another incident took place which brought embarrassment to Colin. Because of the coral make up of the ground, it was not possible to have pit toilets. The principal's house and outhouse were in full view of the girls' dormitory and consequently every effort was made to answer nature's call in the darkness of night. Even then a lamp needed to be carried lest one stood on toads or snakes, which frequented the white coral-lined paths. As an answer to the local situation, a large drum was used to catch and store effluent, and this proved a satisfactory solution.

Until one day, when the container needed emptying. Having arduously dug a hole to bury the waste, Colin lifted the rusting, heavy drum from its position and, hugging it to his chest, he made his way toward the hole. In full view of the girls, he heard giggling and sniggering as they peered out the windows, knowing full well what was in the drum.

It became even more apparent when Colin stubbed his foot on a coral outcrop. As he stumbled, he squeezed the drum even harder and it burst—with the contents showering all over him.

Gales of laughter from the girls' dormitory followed Colin as he made a dash for the basement shower where he endeavoured to thoroughly remove the offending contents of the drum. Nonetheless, Colin was not welcome in the house that night due to an offending odour that was difficult to get rid of.

To Go or Not To Go

* * *

On another occasion, Colin had preached the Sabbath service to a large outdoor audience at a Kainantu district meeting when "nature" started to call. However, all the congregation had to shake hands with the "Big Man" from Lae, so, after the last of more than 1000 hands, he made a hurried trip across the playing field to a "makeshift" leaf and grass toilet.

On entering and seeing it was a squat toilet, he decided to take his trousers off and hang them on a twig. All of a sudden, he felt the floor starting to give way and then a loud crack. He made a grab for the bush wall but to no avail. He found himself in the pit below, trying to keep his shoes out of the mess.

Looking up, all he could see was a mass of women's faces, all chanting, "Sori Master, sori Master." Some strong men appeared and pulled him to solid ground.

One of the older women saw his predicament and handed him a "lap lap"—a loincloth that most island women wear instead of an underskirt.

Colin's trip to the creek was even faster than it had been to the "little house" and someone found him to deliver his salvaged trousers.

A similar thing happened on another occasion. This time a major part of the floor dropped into the pit, but the roof of the toilet collapsed around his ears. So he finished in the pit, covered in leaves and other bush toilet construction materials.

* * *

In 1970, the Winch family was resident in Lae. As dawn was breaking, the family gathered for an early worship and breakfast before Colin was to commence an early flight. As they sat around the table, they heard a scuffle outside and all raced to the window to see what was the cause.

They saw the bare-footed national night-soil man with two full pans connected to a pole supported on his shoulder. He had collected the pans from the toilets of the president and the Winch family. In the process of making his way to the night cart, he had been attacked by Kimi, the Winch family's little dog. The poor man was dancing in circles trying to protect himself from being bitten.

Winchee

Little dogs have a habit of sneaking up behind and nipping the heels of their victim. Kimi was no exception. The Winch children called out to the victim, "Just stand still. He won't hurt you. We will call him!"

The poor fellow responded, "You tink em pussycat. Em no pussycat. Em puppy dog!"

The children collapsed in laughter with the still-frightened man making his exit from the property with Kimi hot on his heels. In vain the children called the dog. It seemed Kimi was having too much fun!

* * *

Toilets on the ground created one type of hazard but when the call of nature occurs while one is in the midst of a flight on a mission plane, logistically the problem takes on a new dimension.

On one occasion, Colin was transporting a boarding-school teacher from Goroka to Mt Hagen. While flying in the beautiful Wahgi Valley, the teacher informed Colin he needed to go to the toilet. Colin assured him that they would be at Mt Hagen within 15 minutes where there was a toilet. The teacher could not wait that long and insisted they land

At the dedication of VH-SDB, (left to right) Pastor Robert Aveling,
Pastor John Lee, Pastor Orm Speck, Ferry Pilot Wayne Fowler,
John Sherriff, Pastor Len Barnard, Pastor Colin Winch.

immediately. Fortunately, there were a number of airstrips along the valley, so Colin obliged by making his approach to the Banz strip.

"Can't you hurry the landing?" queried the distressed passenger. But there was a procedure to be followed. Colin notified Air Control of his change of plans, then circled the airstrip to make sure it was clear of other planes and any local woman walking along the centre of the strip carrying firewood, yams and a *pikinini* (child) on her head. After all, cleared land makes for easier walking as well as for landing of aircraft. He then landed the plane.

"Stop! Stop immediately!" demanded the passenger. It was obvious an embarrassing "accident" was about to happen. Before the plane was at a complete standstill, he leapt from the plane and dashed off into the kunai grass, re-appearing about 15 minutes later with a much-relieved look on his face.

* * *

Flights of longer duration over oceans needed a different solution.

When Colin was flying the twin-engined *J L Tucker* over the Western and Central Pacific area, flights could take as long as six hours between landing places. Sensing a possible problem, Colin contacted supply firms in America. He received a letter from one firm assuring him they had the perfect solution. It consisted of a funnel with a stopper, attached to a long tube that could be fed through a floor vent in the plane to empty the waste underneath and outside the aeroplane.

Then, one morning Colin was mixing powdered milk from an almost empty 3-pound (1.5-kilogram) milk tin when it occurred to him that this empty container would make an ideal receptacle for solid waste. It could even double as a sick bag. Pleased with his thinking, he placed the container under the rear passenger's seat.

On a four-hour flight from Honiara to Nauru, Colin had a union mission officer on board and half-way through the flight the passenger tapped Colin on the shoulder and informed him he needed to answer nature's call.

"No problem! Just feel under your seat and you will find the necessary container," said Colin.

The passenger reached under his seat and pulled out a life-jacket. A

Winchee

second effort resulted in another life-jacket. His third effort brought out the milk tin.

"You don't mean this, do you?" asked the incredulous passenger, noting the confined space within the cabin of the plane.

"Yep! That's it!" was the answer.

The passenger decided to hold on until the plane landed in Nauru. He then half-walked and half-ran with a most unusual gait past the waiting Immigration, Health and Customs authorities to the mens' toilet. Only Colin's explanation of the "emergency" pacified the startled authorities.

Colin replaces the spark plugs on the *Andrew Stewart* while performing a thorough "50 hourly" service at Wirui aerodrome near Wewak, East Sepik District.

Ama Opening

Early in 1966, David Lundstrom arrived at Wewak with his wife, Joyce, and two daughters to begin a three-year term working as the District Director at Ambunti, a small isolated settlement on the northern bank of the mighty Sepik River.

On arrival at Wewak, the family were delighted to renew friendships with Colin and Melva Winch. Colin, Melva and Joyce had trained as nurses together and David had grown up in the Wahroonga area at the time. Awaiting the arrival of their personal effects, the Lundstroms stayed with the Winch family, so naturally conversations took place as to the advantages of mission planes over surface travel.

Earlier in life, David had taken some lessons in flying but did not proceed to pilot status due to shortage of funds to pay for tuition. Needless to say, he shared Colin's enthusiasm for the use of planes in transporting missionaries and supplies throughout New Guinea and determined to look for suitable land for an airstrip in the May River District.

After the Lundstrom's were installed at Ambunti, David prepared for his first patrol to May River aboard the *MV Leleman* in company with mission president, Les Parkinson. The journey motoring against the flow of the Sepik was expected to take three days and several more hours in the swiftly flowing waters of the May River before they reached the May River Government Patrol Post.

Day after day, they passed through low-lying sago swamps as the Sepik snaked its way from mountains to the sea. The waters of the Sepik are brown and silt-laden, while those in the swamps are putrid with rotting vegetation. It was inhospitable countryside for mile after mile, with no visible high land on which to build an airstrip.

On arrival at the patrol post, David noted that the hills dropped sharply into the waters of the river or the sago swamps, again giving no possibility of an airstrip. Visits were made to villages with small groups of Adventist church members along the banks of the upper reaches of

Winchee

the May River, some of which had small schools organised by national teachers.

These were friendly people but many needed medical treatment for infected ulcers, the disfiguring disease of yaws and other maladies. A simple injection of penicillin was the recognised treatment for yaws. David also treated axe wounds and other injuries. He was grateful for the medical instruction he received back in Australia during his term in the army.

A visit to the friendly—but lonely—Australian patrol officer was happily shared by the two missionaries, as well as the officer. He was keen to talk with fellow countrymen. One thing caught David's attention. He was told that patrol officer after patrol officer had searched without success for land on which to locate an airstrip.

Many travelling hours from Ambunti and close to the West Irian border, the inhabitants' staple diet was sago and fish. They were not gardeners. There were a few coconuts growing on the banks of the river and some villagers grew tapioca plants near their huts. Generally, they were only able to find sufficient food for their own purposes.

When a mission worker was located in one of these villages, he would often experience extreme hunger as there was insufficient food to support him. Should such a worker have a family, the situation was perilous and on at least one occasion the child of the family died from hunger. For this and other reasons, access to the area by plane was imperative.

Early in 1967, David was visiting the village of Waniap, located on the side of one of the May River ranges. The hillside plunged into the black waters of Suniap Creek. Meeting with the mission teacher, Noah, and village elders, David asked if they knew of the whereabouts of land sufficiently flat and elevated above the swamp on which to build an airstrip.

After much discussion in their own language, the head man informed David he had been a carrier on a couple of police patrols investigating murders in uncontrolled areas beyond the headwaters of Suniap Creek.

He said there was a village called Ama on high ground "*a long way liklik*" ("quite a way but not too far"). The inhabitants of this village were wild bush people, hunters rather than gardeners, speaking a different language to the May River people.

Ama Opening

It was enough information for David to decide that his next patrol would be into Ama to check out the land.

It was around May, 1967, the expedition began. The Ambunti Mission's 35-foot (10-metre) dugout canoe was packed with supplies, including food for carriers. David made sure he took along a good compass for planning the airstrip, should a suitable location be found.

Realising the danger of entering hostile territory, he refrained from informing his wife of his intention. Having farewelled the family, and accompanied by the national pastor (Pastor Sambale), he set off for Waniap, the canoe being driven by 35-horsepower outboard motor.

On arrival, he selected a guide and suitable carriers, paying the going rate of one shilling per day per carrier, plus food. The carriers were to ride in two village canoes towed behind the mission canoe.

After an early-morning worship and a hearty breakfast, the patrol party excitedly set off in the direction of the headwaters of the Suniap Creek. David was well aware that he was the first missionary to enter the area and, furthermore, he could expect hostility due to the fact the only other outsiders who had preceded him were police searching for a murderer. Local villagers did not appreciate police interference in their lives.

As time went by, the going became more difficult. Trees had fallen into and across the narrowing stream until, just before midday, canoe travel proved impossible, so the trek by land began.

Poles were cut to facilitate the carrying of waterproof boxes, a heavy battery to power the slide projector, the slide projector itself, medical supplies and food—all had to be hoisted onto the backs of the carriers.

The jungle and swamps were alive with leeches. They waited in the grass and on the leaves of trees to latch on to any passer-by from whom they could suck blood, so David had a young boy walk behind him whose sole job was to pull the leeches from David's legs.

With no trail to follow, the guide led the way through virgin forest and swampland, slashing through vines to clear a pathway for the rest of the patrol. It was slow, exhausting work requiring frequent rest-stops in the tropical heat and humidity.

As the afternoon passed, David inquired of the guide, "How much further?"

Winchee

Each time the question was put, the reply came back, *"Close tu lil lik"* ("Not far now").

In mid-afternoon, the group was passing through an incredible forest of mighty trees through which the tropical sun could not penetrate. David and the carriers nervously sensed that they were being watched by hidden warriors, doubtlessly armed with poisoned arrows.

Soon they heard the muffled sound of drums beating out a warning that foreigners were in the area. The jungle telegraph was well and truly alive! Just before darkness fell, they finally broke through the jungle into a clearing and the guide uttered one word: "Ama."

David was faced with a group of naked warriors armed with long bows and an ample supply of arrows. No women or children were to be seen due to the warning given by the beating drums. Because of the lateness of the hour, David urged the guide to endeavour to communicate with the warriors, explaining that the visitors were mission people, not enemies, and that they had come in peace with medicine for the sick and good news to share. He also asked for a place to sleep for the night.

After considerable chatter—none of which David understood—permission was given for them to stay and the group was shown to a thatched hut with two rooms raised from the ground. Worship was held with fervent prayers of thanks to God for His leading and protection, and those appointed to prepare an evening meal set about their task with vigour. All were ravenously hungry so the rice, mixed with canned fish, soon disappeared and the tired patrol group fell into a deep sleep.

* * *

On rising in the morning to the fresh early light, David noted that the women and children had returned and were busy with fire making. Pastor Sambale conducted morning worship and, following breakfast, the whole village was invited to a *tok tok* (meeting).

When about 25 villagers were assembled, David proceeded to hand out gifts to both men and women—bush knives and tomahawks to the men and pretty cloth suitable as wrap-arounds for the women. The joy of the recipients was tangible. A meeting for the evening was announced and offers of medical treatment made.

Ama Opening

Then the main purpose of the visit was explained: the construction of an airstrip should an appropriate strip of land be located. The guide and Pastor Sambale explained the value for them if a *balus* (plane) was able to land in their area, bringing help to their village.

A major breakthrough occurred when two of their younger men stepped forward to enthusiastically explain to the people the advantages of the *balus*. These men had been conscripted to work on a coconut plantation and had flown in an aeroplane. Consequently, the request for land and assistance in clearing the forest was met with an enthusiastic response by the villagers.

David spent some time treating the sick, injecting for yaws, and dressing wounds and infected ulcers. The men of the village were advised that a long length of *Kunda* (Rattan Cane) was required for measuring out the land and when this was attended to the group headed into dense jungle, led by the two enthusiastic men who had already experienced air travel. They followed a trail through the jungle until it came to what had once been a clearing for gardens. Passing through long grass, they again plunged into the jungle, this time without a track to follow.

It was slow going. Undergrowth and clinging vines had to be hacked away by the guides who were moving in a constant direction. Obviously, they knew where they were going. The lack of air movement and tropical humidity sucked energy and the high-pitched screeching of the large cicadas frazzled David's nerves. Still they pressed on until they reached a jungle-covered creek, beyond which was the ever-present swamp.

Now the real task began. The men with the rolled up length of cane were called up with one end placed in the hand of one of them who was told to remain stationary until called forward. The compass was placed in the care of Pastor Sambale who was to keep the advance party on course. This group cleared a path up a slightly rising strip of land with David stepping out 100 paces, then added another 10 for good measure.

At this point, the cane was cut and the man holding the other end at the starting point called up. This method of measurement was repeated 15 times, giving a strip of about 1500 yards (about 1400 metres). There were no discernible humps or hollows in the area and width would be no problem. Final pegs were driven and David was ecstatic. Mission accomplished!

That evening back in the village, David projected slides onto a sheet set up between two stakes. The villagers sat on logs in the centre of the village and made strange noises as each picture was screened—pictures of planes, cars, street scenes, beach scenes and other Papua New Guineans.

The two young men who had experienced these things were excitedly giving a commentary to those who had no idea what lay beyond their forest environment. Little children were running round the back of the sheet to see the pictures on the other side. It was all so new and startling!

Next morning, David and Pastor Sambale left with a promise to return and get the work of clearing the airstrip underway.

They decided to call in on the May River Government Patrol Officer to report on their activities. Expecting a favourable response, David was taken aback when the friendly officer became agitated stating they had no permission to take a patrol into a restricted area. Had they encountered trouble, he would have been responsible to clean up the mess and notify relatives of those killed or wounded.

"On our last police patrol into the Ama area, we had encountered a trap set by the locals who hated the police because they took away their people to jail," he explained. "The villagers had set poisoned-tipped spikes in the mud on the track they knew the police always passed along. Those in the police contingent who did not wear heavy boots were badly injured, and the patrol had to be aborted and return for medical treatment."

Hearing this, both David and Pastor Sambale knew they had been divinely protected, especially David who had tramped to Ama barefooted.

Asking for and receiving forgiveness, David and Pastor Sambale headed home in the mission canoe—a trip hastened by the flow of the rivers.

It was a joyful reunion with the great news being shared. Joyce was thrilled to listen to the details of the trip over the special meal she prepared for her loved one. And David was happily feasting on long-awaited home-cooking.

Ama Opening

* * *

Colin was also delighted to hear the news, as was Pastor Lionel Smith, the newly appointed Sepik Mission president. An airstrip at Ama would be both cost-saving and time-saving for the work of the church. The journey that would then take more than two days by mission canoe would take about 35 minutes flying from Ambunti to Ama. Using Ama as a base, the whole of the May River area could be reached quickly and efficiently.

First, however, the land had to be cleared. This included felling huge trees and clearing dense undergrowth. Tools would be needed, including axes, picks, mattocks, spades, shovels and bush knives. These were approved by the Sepik Mission committee so clearing could begin. A budget was approved for a national worker to be located at Ama to work with the villagers on the project. The initial airdrop of these tools was achieved as Colin made a number of low-level passes over the village with David pushing the equipment out of the open doorway.

In 1968, David made several trips to Ama, realising the task was beyond the ability of the local people with only basic tools available to them. They had done a magnificent job felling many of the huge trees but these lay where they fell, many more than 100 feet (30 metres) in length. They needed to be cut up and fires built around the stumps, no bulldozer being available in that remote forest region.

He decided to buy a chainsaw with a 3-foot (90-centimetre) blade, using this to cut the huge logs into manageable lengths to roll away from the clearing. A new, all-aluminium De Havilland River Truck, powered by a 50 horsepower outboard motor had been brought for the May River area. This shallow-draught workhorse could carry around one ton and still cut the travel time to the May River by a third.

Using this boat, David took a team of nationals with him and stayed at Ama for a time, spending the daylight hours carving up the jungle. Even Pastor Lionel Smith, the Sepik Mission president, spent time at Ama helping with the clearing work.

Excitement mounted.

Work continued day after day, encouraged by the presence of the two Australians and the two other visiting national team members. After

Winchee

some days, the visitors had to return to their other duties, leaving the locals to keep up the momentum.

Months went by and David patrolled again into Ama to check on progress, happily reporting back to Colin that he thought an initial landing was possible.

* * *

Joyce Lundstrom takes up the story:

"Sierra Delta Bravo—circuit area Ama." The voice of missionary pilot Pastor Colin Winch came faintly from my radio. They were there above Ama! Would the strip be ready? Would they land?

Sitting beside the radio, I could picture the scene with the little red-and-white plane circling the newly-cut airstrip deep in the jungle of the May River area. I imagined the excitement on the ground below as the people watched and waited; and the uncertainty in the plane as around and around they went. Will we try it? I knew that Pastor Winch would not land if there appeared to be any patch that did not look good, but from the plane no-one could see how soft the ground was.

It was October 21, 1969, and the plane had come, permission for the initial landing had been given and the plane was circling as three pairs of eyes searched the ground for likely "bad spots." With Pastor Winch was Pastor Lionel Smith and my husband. They had left our mission station at Ambunti 35 minutes earlier with a load of cargo to do an airdrop, but they had discussed the possibility of landing if the strip looked good—and that was what I was anxious about.

My husband had visited the strip a few weeks earlier and he felt confident that the little jobs remaining to be done had been done, but who can be sure until those wheels touched the ground?

"Sierra Delta Bravo," my thoughts were jerked back to the radio as I waited with bated breath. "Am going in for initial landing. Will report on the ground."

I had the answer to my question. They were going down. "Dear Lord," I prayed, "Watch over them and keep them safe. May the ground be firm and smooth."

In my anxiety, I could imagine what was taking place: the decision to land had been made, a prayer for guidance would be said, and Pastor Winch would be busy bringing the plane down over the treetops in line with the strip, throttle back and lowering the flaps to slow the speed, as slowly, carefully the wheels would come lower and lower toward that patch of ground that somehow would suddenly appear to be nowhere near long enough or smooth enough. I knew that inside the plane the tenseness

The newly opened Ama airstrip was hacked from extremely thick rain forest.

would match my own as I waited for five long fear-filled minutes.

"Sierra Delta Bravo. On the ground at Ama," the quiet voice said, almost casually. Thank You, God. They were down safely!

Imagine the excitement of the local people as they saw the plane coming lower and lower, touching down and rolling to a stop. At last they see the reward for their labours and the plane actually on the ground beside them.

Imagine the joy of the national worker and his young family as they saw the plane on the ground and knew they were not so isolated anymore! Imagine the terror and pride of the headman and the wails of his wife and children as, after Pastor Winch does a solo takeoff to try the strip, he took the headman for a circuit of the area.

Imagine, too, my fear as sometime later I once more hear the familiar call, "Sierra Delta Bravo. Taxiing Ama for Ambunti," and I knew they were preparing to come home. I knew the danger there was in lifting the three of them off. Had the approaches been cut far enough back to allow the plane to get altitude before the trees blocked the airspace? "Dear Lord, Lift them off. Send the angels to lift them over the trees!"

Then imagine my thankfulness and relief as again the calm voice crackled into the room, "Sierra Delta Bravo. Left Ama—airborne!"

In 35 minutes they would be safely back in Ambunti, leaving behind them in the jungle the assurance that a better and happier way of life was starting, that medical help would be coming to heal their sores and diseases, and that their babies need not die through ignorance and malnutrition.

Information for this chapter was supplied by David Lundstrom, who also graciously gave access to articles written by his deceased wife, Joyce.

Landing on a Band-aid

David Lunstrom and Colin had spent the Sabbath at Telefomin visiting with the Adventists in the area. It was Sunday morning and they were due to return to their respective mission stations to take up the duties of the new week, David at Ambunti and Colin at Maprik.

On arrival at the airstrip in preparation for their flight, they found one tyre on the *Andrew Stewart* was completely flat.

There were no tools on the plane to care for such an emergency, so the men went to the local Public Works Department offices to see if help was available in the form of tools, patches and a vulcaniser. Unfortunately no patches were available, new supplies being on order, but they were able to help with wheel-stud sockets. Next call was to the local Kiap who lent them a screwdriver and a jack. The plane was tilted by men lifting on the wing struts, and chocks put in place to enable the wheel to be removed.

Being a split rim, the removal of the tube involved more work than on a one-piece rim. When the tube was removed, the puncture was located but there seemingly was no means of repair available. Silently Colin offered a prayer of thanks to God for His protection.

Being a practical man, David recalled the time he was clearing land along the banks of the Murchison River in Western Australia and a tyre was punctured in his utility. At that time, he successfully temporarily repaired the puncture using band-aids, He was confident he could do the same with the aeroplane tube.

Carefully, they cleaned the tube with alcohol before adhering two large band-aids, one on top of the other, over the hole. After pumping up the tube and submerging it in water, they found it was holding

Winchee

pressure, so it was returned with its tyre to the split wheel, the wheel bolts were tightened and lock-wired and the wheel secured to the undercarriage.

The tyre was pumped up to the correct pressure, which was monitored several times every five minutes to satisfy Colin that it was holding the pressure. Then the borrowed tools were returned to their respective owners and Colin informed David he did not want to risk two landings on such temporary repairs, so he would land on the Wirui airstrip just out of Wewak and replace the punctured tube before heading back to Ambunti.

Soon they were in the air on their way to Wewak.

Not wanting to risk undue pressure on the faulty tyre, Colin decided to land the *Andrew Stewart* on one wheel, only lowering the faulty wheel to the airstrip after touch down. Obviously this involved a great deal of skill and—for David, at least—a degree of tension. But the manoeuvre

A local missionary helps Colin replace the *Andrew Stewart*'s wheel after repairing the tube with several strips of sticking plaster.

Landing on a Band-aid

was completed successfully, increasing David's already high evaluation of Colin as a pilot.

The tube replaced, they flew on to Ambunti but the incident remains fixed in David's memory as a day never to be forgotten.

Foot-slogging Among the Kukukukus

It was 1968 and the Winch family was located at Kainantu. The *Malcolm Abbott* was Colin's pride and joy. But Colin had other aspects of missionary outreach on his mind. He was planning another 16-day patrol to the villages in the Kukukuku Mountains. Welfare bags had been dropped into the area and Colin had completed a previous patrol into the area with Hugh Dickens, so the villagers had some prior knowledge of this strange white man whose road was the skies.

Colin knew that Tony Voigt, an agriculturalist from Australia, was working at Kabiufa and invited him to join the patrol. With some reluctance, Tony was given permission and gladly accepted the opportunity to see for himself these small but feared warriors.

Only bare necessities could be taken as they would be scrambling up and down slippery mountain trails and crossing raging streams by means of native-built bridges. Each had a blow-up mattress, a plate, a spoon and a small washbowl big enough to hold a half-gallon (2 litres) of water.

National carriers would carry the all-important picture roll and hand-grinder made into a generator for showing filmstrips, also bags of salt from which they would be paid their wages and, where necessary, could be traded for food from the village gardens.

Tony was aware that Colin was extremely particular in planning such events, and had a reputation for safety when it came to loads carried by

Foot-slogging Among the Kukukukus

air. He refused point blank to overload any plane he was flying and thus was highly respected as a pilot throughout Papua New Guinea.

Having farewelled their families and committed the patrol to the care of the Almighty, the two men boarded the *Malcolm Abbott* and flew to Wonenara, gateway to Kukukuku country, where they locked the plane, tying it down to await their return.

Having arranged for their carriers and a translator, the party set out on the 10-hour hike to Wantikia. Up and up they climbed, often having to drag themselves forward by pulling on tree roots or bushes. It was lung-busting work.

Having reached almost 9000 feet (2700 metres), they then had to scramble down the steep, slippery mountainside. Ascent was easier on the legs than descent. Soon both missionaries experienced shin soreness.

When they came to a roaring mountain stream, they noted that the

VH-SDB about to be backed into a corner of the Wonenara airstrip parking area awaiting Colin's return from a 16-day "walkabout patrol" through the Kukukuku Mountains.

Winchee

only way across was by a slender fallen tree linking the two banks some 15 feet (4.5 metres) above the water. Tony did not like heights and Colin's reaction was not much different.

But both men knew they had to make the crossing, and suffered from an instant inferiority complex as they saw the carriers nonchalantly run across the slippery log. All the missionaries could do was shuffle across, their hearts in their mouths until they reached solid ground. The crossing was the occasion for great mirth among the carriers as they sat around the fire that night.

Disregarding fatigue, worship was held in Wantikia village that evening. The picture roll was brought out and simple gospel stories told. Villagers everywhere loved the picture roll. The filmstrips were also a big hit.

Children everywhere love games and Tony became their favourite as he performed a trick for them. He would slap himself on the back of the head and, at that same instant the top plate of his false teeth would pop out. The children's eyes boggled. They knew nothing about false teeth and nor did their parents.

"*Gen, gen!*" ("Again, again!") they shouted They even slapped themselves on the back of their heads but no teeth popped out.

Tony did it again . . . and again . . . and again!

After a late meal that night, the two missionaries slept in the *house Kiap* (Government officer's hut). It had been a long, hard day.

* * *

The next morning the patrol left Wantikia for the nine-hour hike to Simbari. Stiff muscles protested the exercise but more heights of 9000 feet lay ahead. Wantikia lies at about 5000 feet (1500 metres) so the actual climbs were some 4000 feet (1200 metres).

The hike was again made up of ascents and descents on slippery, muddy trails. Though both men wore boots with canvas leggings, they still were attacked by leeches and when they removed their boots at night, not only were their socks wet and muddy, but also red with blood. It was normal for any patrol in Papua New Guinea.

The hard rubber-soled boots of the missionaries were not ideal for hard slippery surfaces. The carriers, however, were bare-footed. Their

Foot-slogging Among the Kukukukus

broad flat feet stuck like limpets to a rock as the crossed the log-bridges.

As the day progressed, it was not unusual, on descent, to see the next village in a blue haze across the valley through a gap in the trees. It could take another three or four hours before reaching it, as a steep descent, the crossing of another stream, followed by an equally steep ascent had to be made.

On arrival at Simbari, the patrolling party found the village almost deserted. The women were out working in the gardens and the men were hunting. Neither would return until dusk when meal preparation would begin.

Tony noted that the protein-starved Kukukukus seemed to eat "anything that moved!" The men had become experts with bow and arrow from childhood and returned with cuscus (mouse possum), large bush rats, birds, caterpillars and beetles. All were considered good food. The women had brought *kaukau* (sweet potatoes), taro and kumu (a green leafy vegetable, somewhat similar to spinach) from the gardens.

Tony noted that the men would dip the cuscus in the flames, singeing off the fur, then gnaw the almost-raw flesh. Though pigs were plentiful, they were only killed and eaten on ceremonial occasions. The missionaries had brought packets of dried soup with them and traded salt for sweet potatoes, passing on the caterpillars. It was not restaurant-level cuisine but filled empty bellies.

Worship was held once more and again there was rapt attention as the plan of salvation was told, illustrated by the picture roll and the filmstrips. It was thrilling to see the changes made in the lives of these former cannibals. As hearts were surrendered to the Lord Jesus, immediate changes were made in individual lives and shame was expressed for their cannibalistic past.

Again, Tony made friends with the children by popping out his teeth. Even some of the adults stood in wonderment, trying to replicate the act without success. To them it was *"wokim puripuri"* (magic). A welcome sleep ended the day!

* * *

Each day, Colin and Tony debriefed the previous day's activity and planned the day ahead. On the third day, the plan was to tramp

Winchee

from Simbari to Mineri—a hike of about seven hours over rugged mountainous country with heights of up to 9800 feet (almost 3000 metres). At these high altitudes, breathing becomes laboured and one needs to take occasional rests. Fortunately, both men were somewhat acclimatised in that their homes were at 5000 feet (1500 metres).

Nevertheless the climb in the existing conditions was gut-wrenching. Rain was a constant factor in the Highlands of Papua New Guinea. Consequently, the trails were always muddy and slippery. This was yet another day of ascents, log bridges over thundering mountain streams, and descents, each activity repeated a number of times. Tony developed a deep respect for the carriers who took it all in their stride, as if it were a daily happening.

The evening in Mineri followed the same pattern as in the previous villages. Again the picture roll attracted the villagers as Colin, through the interpreter, told the gospel story. Colin has always been known as the master storyteller and his ability to hold an audience of Kukukuku villagers was a real eye-opener to Tony.

In one village, they met an Afro-American and a white man, translators representing the New Tribes Mission who had dedicated two years of their lives to living with the Kukukuku tribesmen. Religious differences were not featured as any meeting between people of the same language was always a highlight to be looked forward to in the remote vastness of this land. Their dedication left a lasting impression on Colin and Tony.

The patrol took them from village to village, with the missionaries spending a night in each village before retracing their steps to the aeroplane at Wonenara. The ascents became descents and the descents were ascents as they tramped their way homeward

Glad to be home, they thanked the Lord for His protection and care, asking for a blessing on each village in which they had ministered. For Tony the whole experience had been eye-opening. As he re-evaluated what was important in his life, material things lost much of their glamour. He returned to his post of duty, thanking the Lord for the privilege of what he had witnessed.

Flying Fish and Wandering Feet

Pastor Ron Vince had come from the Division headquarters in Wahroonga at the time Colin was doing a flight from Wewak to Pagi on the West Irian border. So Colin invited Ron to join him on the flight. Colin was transporting boxes of Bibles and food supplies to the national workers who had been located there to open up the work in that area. Bags of rice and cartons of tinned fish would help keep these workers going until they established their gardens in the villages to which they had been appointed.

It was a lovely morning for flying up the northwest coast of Papua New Guinea before heading inland for Pagi. Both men were enjoying the flying conditions as they chatted. Colin explained to Ron how easy it was to fly the plane. He then offered the controls to Ron, explaining the uses of the different control mechanisms. With these explanations, he gave demonstrations of each of the controls.

Ron was delighted to accept the offer and, for a time, flew along quite acceptably. Then something must have startled him because, all of a sudden, he pushed hard on the control column.

The aeroplane nose dropped and for an instant the plane was weightless and a carton of tinned fish in the back cargo compartment rose into the air and hovered until Colin resumed control of the plane. It then crashed down on the bags of rice. While the load had been secured, it had obviously not been secured sufficiently. They had produced another type of "flying fish"!

* * *

Winchee

On another occasion, Colin was flying out of Wewak's Wirui airstrip with an American church worker, who showed intense interest in photographing all he was seeing. It was all so new and different.

Anticipating a problem, Colin took time to explain the confined space within the cockpit of the small aeroplane and therefore the close proximity to vital instrumentation. The visitor was seated in the right-hand front seat and warned to be careful not to touch the rudder pedals or the control column as he moved to take pictures.

After a prayer for the Lord's protection, Colin taxied to the end of the runway in preparation for takeoff, notified traffic control of the flight details and gunned the engine, gathering speed down the runway. The nose of the aeroplane had lifted and the pilot was about to lift the rear wheels when suddenly, with no warning, the plane veered sharply to the left, heading for a road that ran parallel to the runway.

Glancing at the rudder pedals, Colin noted his passenger had his left shoe pushed hard against the left pedal. The passenger had seen something flashing past that he wished to photograph and, swivelling in his seat, had shot out his leg to stabilise himself, not realising he had placed his foot on the left rudder pedal.

There was no time for niceties.

Colin gave the American a thump on his left leg to alert him to what he had done, and fought with the controls to avoid the impending crash. Just in the nick of time, Colin regained control of the plane and brought it back to the centre line of the runway. It was a quiet passenger who sat still in his seat for the rest of the flight!

Search-and-Rescue Missions

On many occasions, mission planes were called out by the Department of Civil Aviation to assist in searching for missing, presumed-crashed aircraft. Most years in Papua New Guinea—and on rarer occasions in the Solomon Islands—an aeroplane would go missing and all charter operators and mission pilots with available planes would be called out to search for the downed pilot and passengers.

Usually these incidents would occur in bad weather and mostly along the mountainous spine of New Guinea, which rises up to 15,000 feet (4500 metres) and in West Irian to 17,000 feet (more than 5000 metres). Sometimes pilots were caught in clouds and would try to climb out, only to be snagged by some limestone ridge. There were instances where pilots lost their radio and, without being able to communicate to base, had landed on some isolated strip, thus triggering an organised search.

The Department of Civil Aviation would initiate certain phases. If a pilot did not call in at the time nominated for his position or landing report, an "uncertainty phase" would be raised. After half an hour, if there was no response from the pilot to the many pilots calling him, a more urgent phase would be initiated. On the other hand, if a pilot had called in notifying of an engine failure, a "distress phase" would immediately be set in motion. Under such circumstances, the plane in distress would sometimes crash into the huge canopy of tropical jungle and settle below the closed-over canopy, making it difficult to be seen from the air.

Two types of aerial search followed. The Department of Civil

Winchee

Aviation would allocate given areas to each search pilot, together with his spotters. Initially it would involve a relatively elevated grid search. Grid lines would be followed accurately, back and forward—north to south, east to west, covering an allocated area.

For both pilot and spotters, this was a tiring process. Keeping one's eyes fixed on rugged mountains or dense foliage while looking for any glint of sunshine on metal, white twisted wreckage, or broken branches as evidence of a crashed aircraft, was a strain upon the senses.

Then came contour searching. This was more dangerous for pilot and spotters, having been given a base altitude and a peak altitude between which they would search. Starting at the highest designated altitude, the pilot would follow the contours of the mountains, sometimes into tight valleys. He needed to be very alert as he flew the aeroplane at little above stalling speed, constantly aware that at any

The crew and observers for the search and rescue of the local trading boat *MV Mussira*: (left to right) WPUM president Pastor Gordon Lee, Melva, Colin and Pastor John Kosmeier, local mission president.

Search-and-Rescue Missions

moment he may have to give full throttle to pull out of a potentially dangerous situation. Having completed one run, he would turn in the opposite direction giving the spotters on the other side of the plane the opportunity to use their rested eyes once more.

Should nothing be spotted, the pilot would descend a couple of hundred feet and repeat the process until the whole designated area was covered. Of course, each pilot had also to be alert that he did not fly into the path of another searching plane covering an adjacent area.

These searches would often go for hour after hour, sometimes requiring the pilot to land the plane for refuelling, during which food and hot drinks would be consumed before returning to the air once more. A tremendous effort was always made to find the downed aviator and his passengers. Sometimes days of searching took place before the lost was found and most often the downed pilot and any passengers were killed in the crash. It then became a case of retrieval of the bodies.

With a broken engine, the lost *MV Mussira*'s crew tried to set up a sail with a tarpaulin.

Winchee

* * *

But not all search-and-rescue operations took place over land. There were times also when mission planes were asked to search for a lost or disabled ship.

Gordon Lee and Colin had been holding district meetings at Boliu, Mussau Island, while the *J L Tucker* had been parked on a wartime airstrip at Emirau. On arrival back on the morning of April 19, 1971, they were notified that an inter-island trading vessel, the *Mussira*, was missing at sea somewhere north of Emirau, having lost power and also with no radio contact. The *Malalagi* had already set out to sea to endeavour to locate the stricken vessel. But the Papua New Guinea Search-and-Rescue authorities requested Colin to make an aerial search. Colin was familiar with the *Mussira* as, during his residency at Boliu, the captain had kindly brought much longed-for mail and groceries to the isolated family.

They searched for some time without success and, running short of fuel, were forced to return to Kavieng to replenish the tanks. Again they took off, Melva Winch, Gordon Lee and John Kosmier being the spotters, while Colin concentrated on flying.

Eventually they located the missing vessel drifting far to the northwest, some 65 nautical miles (120 kilometres) from Kavieng. There was little or no hope of the boat touching land, even though they had caught a glimpse of Tench Island in the distance. Some of the crew could be seen swimming in the water, vainly endeavouring to tow the heavy vessel to the island. It was a losing battle.

Unable to make radio contact, Colin flew low over the *Mussira* as Gordon Lee wrote a message on John Kosmier's rubber thong (flip-flop), notifying the crew that the *Malalagi* was searching for them and that the plane would lead it to them. They would be towed to safety.

The thong was thrown from the plane and landed alongside the *Mussira*. It was recovered from the sea, the message read and acknowledged.

Colin then flew to the *Malalagi*, where another thong was dropped giving the location of the stricken vessel and instructions to follow the direction the plane flew in order to meet up with the *Mussira*. So continued the journey to reach the stricken vessel.

Search-and-Rescue Missions

For five hours, the *J L Tucker* flew between the two vessels until the *Mussira* was taken in tow back to Kavieng. Total flying time in the rescue effort was seven hours and 10 minutes.

This rescue won accolades from the Chinese owners of the *Mussira*, as well as from the government. Thereafter, generous donations were given to Gordon Lee as he called on the boat owners each year on the annual mission appeal and freight was carried free of charge to the mission stations.

A message on a rubber thong about to be dropped to the crew below.

The Day God Spoke

June 1, 1966, had been a busy day for Colin, having flown from Goroka to Kainantu and then to Lae, where he spent time shopping before taking passengers and goods to Menyama late in the afternoon. It was a bumpy flight and despite solid cross winds, Colin made a safe landing and quickly unloaded passengers and goods.

Nightfall was one hour away and the flight time from Menyama to Kainantu was 35 minutes. Colin anticipated this would give him plenty of time for the last flight of the day. He re-started the engine and made a careful pre-flight check of all instruments, before notifying Flight Control at Lae that he was about to take off for Kainantu.

The weather around the mountains of Papua New Guinea can change quickly and dramatically, and the best time for flying is early in the morning. By mid-afternoon, heavy cloud and thunderstorms can build up producing rain squalls and poor visibility, making flying hazardous. When flying in adverse weather, it is always wise to have the option of aborting the flight and returning to the point of departure. Pilots describe this as keeping the back door open. It is critical that such a decision be made at the most appropriate moment.

Without passengers or cargo on board, the *Malcolm Abbott* leaped quickly into the air and a left-hand turn took Colin out of the Menyama Valley. He set course to the north for Kainantu, planning to cross the Kratke Mountains, which rose to a height above 11,600 feet (3500 metres).

This was not the usual route he would take but because night was coming on and the plane was load-free, he made this choice. On reaching 7000 feet (2100 metres) while climbing out of the Menyama Valley, he noticed a huge thunderhead capping the mountains. Seeking to circumnavigate this threatening weather and the mountain range, Colin veered slightly to the right, levelling off at 7000 feet.

While flying northward in smooth air and clear visibility, he noted the cloud above billowing up to join the huge, well-developed thunderhead.

The Day God Spoke

He continued to fly around the mountain range and clear of the ridges that ran down to the Markham River, having visible evidence that the sun was shining on Kunai Hills ahead.

Every now and then Colin turned the plane 30 or 40 degrees so he could look back from the direction in which he had come to ensure he had a safe exit if needed. So far, so good and so he proceeded on toward Kainantu, even though it became very dark.

The sunshine ahead lured him on but the lightning was flashing and he heard the claps of thunder above the roar of the engine. The lowering clouds began to cause Colin to decrease his elevation toward the ridges but still giving sufficient clearance for him to get through.

There was a mighty flash of lightning with an instantaneous boom of thunder, which shook the plane in the ensuing wind and turbulence.

Down came the rain! On checking, Colin saw his back-door escape had suddenly been closed by heavy rain and lowering, angry black clouds. He had been caught!

The heaviest rain he had ever seen beat on the outer aluminium shell of the little aeroplane, creating a horrific din.

"Lord, I've been foolish," Colin prayed. "Please help me out of this situation!"

There was no alternative but to keep flying toward Kainantu. He did not dare climb up through the cloud because of the severe turbulence and the surrounding mountain peaks. Visibility was deteriorating and he was forced down near the ridges and into the valleys.

Normally on this route, Colin had flown higher but, from this low elevation, the landscape took on a different appearance. Hillocks that had seemed so small from the higher altitude now appeared as mountains.

"Lord, help me," he prayed again. "I need Your help. Please help me."

Even though the sun had not set, because of the heavy rain and huge cloud it was as dark as night.

Instrument lights were turned on and he continued to fly on, weaving through the valleys and hopping across ridges, then down into the next valley. Because Colin had flown to the right around the Kratke Range, he was sure Kainantu was slightly to his left. The Kunai ridges looked familiar to him. The mountains were awash with water.

Winchee

Waterfalls were tumbling down just off his wing tips—an incredible sight to see.

He continued to fly with limited visibility. He was in a serious situation and tension was mounting. Any moment he could run out of space and crash into a mountainside. His thoughts went to his family and in desperation he prayed more: "Lord! Help me!"

At that moment, Colin felt a deep impression that someone was sitting beside him in the right-hand seat. The impression was so strong he looked and put out his hand—but felt nothing! Still, he was sure someone was sitting there with him.

Then he heard what seemed to be a voice say, "Turn to the right!"

He knew that was wrong. "Lord! I know Kainantu is to the left, not to the right," he said out loud. "I'll just fly down this little valley and I think I'll run into it!"

He flew into the valley with the rain bucketing down on the fuselage and the plane bucking and jumping in the wind as it funnelled down the narrow valley and over the ridges.

Kainantu was not down that valley.

Again, "Lord! Help me. Please help me!"

And then that voice once more, "Turn to the right. Turn to the right!"

By this time, the usually composed pilot was terrified. He was looking death in the face! "Alright, Lord!" he said. "I'll turn right—but Kainantu isn't there."

He turned and flew to his right. As he banked, he spied a light below. By now Colin was well overdue and the Control Centre at Lae was calling. Last light was approaching rapidly. Where Colin was, last light had already fallen!

But there was a light—and another light. Then Colin saw the lights of cars driving on the Highlands Highway. Just under his left wing were the lights of the Lutheran Mission, just 3 miles (5 kilometres) from Kainantu. He had passed Kainantu and would have been spot-on if he had turned when he first heard the voice.

Relieved and humbled, he flew over the Kainantu airstrip and Pastor Rex Tindall's home, revving the motor to let him know the mission plane had arrived. As he made his final approach, Colin made a radio call to the Lae Control Centre, notifying them he was in the

The Day God Spoke

circuit area at Kainantu and to cancel his search-and-rescue watch.

He landed the *Malcolm Abbott* in the heavy rain with water spraying up over the plane as his wheels touched the gravel airstrip. He was safe!

"Thank You, Lord," he prayed. "Thank you for helping this ignorant and stubborn pilot!"

Chris and Colin beside the mission plane at Kainantu, Eastern Highlands.

Held Aloft in Angel's Hands

It was a cool crisp Highlands morning. Colin, Melva, and their four children, Kerry, Carol, Nerolie and small son, Chris, were based at Kainantu, a small town exactly a mile high (about 1600 metres) in the Eastern Highlands of Papua New Guinea. For some weeks, Colin had been planning to fly over the Kukukuku Mountains to drop bags of welfare clothing into each of 12 villages in the area. This was to be the day!

As part of the plan, a request had been sent to each resident missionary to prepare a list of the elderly, young children and babies in each village so appropriate clothing could be packed into each wheat bag to meet the needs of those most vulnerable, such as those suffering from lung infections due to the cold nights experienced in the Highlands.

Once filled, each bag was sewn up with the name of the village printed in large letters near the top. These bags had been loaded into the Cessna 180 after removing the centre and back seats, as well as the passenger-side door. This was done to facilitate the exit of the bag from the plane. Experience had shown that ejecting bags through the window had proved problematic to the critical timing of the drop.

Colin waited for a New Guinea teacher to arrive who had agreed to sit in the "air conditioned" seat and dispense the bags. Apparently his courage had deserted him and he failed to turn up.

Colin then went searching for Oeva, the groundsman of the Kainantu mission station, who had been pestering for months for his first ride in the aeroplane. When asked if he would like the opportunity, he answered by jumping into the front seat of the Landrover, beaming from ear to ear.

Held Aloft in Angel's Hands

Until he noticed the door of the Cessna in the back!

Colin parked the vehicle near the aeroplane and walked to the plane to check the load was secure. On turning to speak to Oeva, he saw him hightailing it up the road back to the mission station. His excitement had disappeared when he saw the gaping doorway in the side of the plane! It was not possible for the pilot to fly the plane and eject the bags at the same time. A second person had to be involved.

After a considerable amount of pleading, Oeva agreed to assist, even though he was aware they would be flying into the feared Kukukuku country. He was from a village on the edge of the Kukukuku Mountains and his people were afraid of these small warriors, who were feared throughout Papua New Guinea because they had the reputation of eating their enemies.

"What if *Pasta Winis* (Pastor Winch) decided to land on the airstrip in the middle of cannibal country. Would I be eaten?" he asked.

It took much courage to put aside his fears. Colin helped Oeva up into the "ventilated" seat, securing the safety harness around him. They practised the ejection process a few times to be sure Oeva understood what was required of him.

He was asked if he was OK and replied, "*Mi redi!*" ("I am ready!").

After one last check of the plane and a prayer for God's protection, the propeller made a half turn and the engine burst into life. Lae Control was notified by radio of the flight into the Kukukuku Mountains as the Cessna taxied down the runway.

Little did either of the men realise that the angels had begun their care at that moment.

The throb of the engine and the wind-rush from the propeller roared into the cabin, startling Oeva and causing him to lean heavily against the pilot. Colin gave him a gentle jab in the ribs to straighten him up, explaining that no pilot could fly a plane with a passenger lying on him.

Being his first flight, Oeva had no comprehension of the power of wind. He was to experience even greater noise and the force of the disturbed air as the throttle was opened at the end of the airstrip. The blast caused eddies of dust to rise off the cockpit floor and from the bags.

Again, Oeva shrank from the fury of the blast and leaned heavily on

Winchee

Colin, but a gentle dig in the ribs from Colin's elbow reminded him to sit up straight.

Gathering speed down the runway, the Cessna 180 lifted into the clear morning air, glistening in the sun as it clawed its way into the sky, with its heavy load. The destination was to the south so the first turn was to the right.

As the plane banked, Oeva was hanging in his safety harness looking, with unrestricted view, through the open doorway. He screamed at the top of his voice. Startled, Colin thought he had panicked but this was not the case. Down below was the Highlands Highway, on which a moving jeep could be seen. Oeva had spotted some of his friends on board and was calling to them to look up at him.

In his excitement, he pushed his hand out into the air stream to wave to them, only to have it slapped to the side of the doorway by the force of the wind. Giving his hand a rub, he wondered what it was that had

Oeva, the mission station gardener, learns the technique of aerial dropping. He became Colin's best drop-master.

the power to force his hand like that. It was all such a new experience.

Having climbed into the cold air at 10,000 feet (about 3000 metres) to clear the Marawaka Gap, Colin throttled back a little and descended into the warmer Marawaka Valley. The throttle was to be a vital part of the day's flying, but Colin was totally unaware he was using a "time bomb." He noted out of the corner of his eye that Oeva was tentatively extending his arm out of the plane, playing with the slip stream, also totally unaware that at any second his life could end.

The missionaries in each village had been advised the drop would be on this day and all villagers had been told to retreat to their houses when the mission plane flew over. While every attempt was made for an accurate drop, this did not always occur. On one occasion, a bag had crashed through the leaf roof of a jungle home. Fortunately, the occupants were not injured.

To carry out the exercise successfully, there needed to be precise timing between the pilot and the one ejecting the bags.

Colin made frequent use of the throttle to warn the residents of the impending drop, then throttled back as the plane descended and, with full flaps down, slowed to the point of the drop, before accelerating again as it climbed and proceeded over the ridge to the next village. This procedure was followed over all 12 villages, opening and closing the throttle numerous times. Colin was totally unaware that a serious problem was imminent.

The task successfully completed, Colin waggled the wings in farewell and returned to Kainantu where he revved the engine to alert Melva that he was home, closed the throttle at 500 feet (150 metres) and landed, with Oeva grinning from ear to ear. What a story he had to tell to his village mates that night around the fire!

* * *

A few days later, Eddie Piez, secretary–treasurer of the Papua New Guinea Union Mission, was planning to take a commercial flight to Mt Hagen. On hearing this, Colin suggested a saving could be made if Eddie chose to join him in his flying activities on that day. Colin was to fly from Lae to Usarumpia to pick up an American volunteer missionary and his wife, Bill and Joyce Cochran, who had been sharing

Winchee

the gospel in remote villages in the Kukukuku Mountains. They were to be taken to Kainantu. The flight would then continue on to Karamui before making the final leg into Mt Hagen. Eddie happily agreed to the suggestion, realising he would save funds and at the same time see some of the remote Highlands areas.

Following prayer for a safe flight, they left Lae, observing that the mountains in their direction of travel were unusually clear. Eddie tended to suffer from motion sickness but on this flight the problem was eliminated when Colin handed over the controls once the plane was airborne. Clear skies sometimes herald strong winds and this proved true as they approached Usarumpia.

The Usarumpia airstrip is on the side of a mountain. It is reached by flying down the Marawaka Valley, then turning right into a smaller offshoot valley, on the side of which is the airstrip with bush-clad mountains close by on either side. Once the last half of the final approach is reached, there is no turning back. It is land or crash.

The short strip is on a steep incline, varying from 10 to 16 degrees with a level turning platform at the top. Taking over the controls, Colin made the approach in strong crosswinds. Once the wheels settled on the ground, he opened the throttle increasing power to make the incline to where the passengers were waiting, together with many local people. Eddie marvelled that anyone would consider making a landing strip in such formidable surroundings.

Following loading and another prayer for safety, the group took off down the steep slope and became airborne in time to look down on the sheer drop into the valley below. In flight, Colin and Eddie discussed the twin-engined Aztec plane donated by the Quiet Hour in America being converted to Australian standards at Aiyura. They decided to drop in and see how the work was progressing. Again the landing was made in strong crosswinds but Colin was experienced in such conditions and used the throttle extensively to counter the winds.

After a brief stay, they took off for the two-minute flight to Kainantu. The Cessna 180 is a dual-control aeroplane. The wild winds buffeted the plane necessitating Colin having control, though Eddie had his hands on the dual controls, giving him the sense of flying the plane as a prevention of airsickness. The plane was positioned for final approach

Held Aloft in Angel's Hands

and Eddie was asked to lower the flaps and check that the throttle was closed. It was not!

Something was dramatically wrong. Colin noted that they were overshooting slightly. He took control and landed the plane safely, rolling past the taxiway. After an initial check of the problem, they exited the aeroplane and pushed it back into the parking bay.

On checking further, Colin pulled the throttle cable out of its outer cable, finding it had worn so badly it had been only hanging by a thread. It had finally broken some time on the short two-minute flight into Kainantu.

The flying conditions on that day had necessitated an extensive use of the throttle. Had it broken on the approach to or takeoff from Usarumpia, it would have meant certain death. But it broke on approach to landing at Kainantu.

Both men gave thanks as they considered the day's use of the throttle The Lord's "everlasting arms" were certainly underneath them that day.

And after all that, Eddie took a commercial flight from Kainantu to Mt Hagen.

Night Flight

The Papuan Gulf Mission committee meetings were being held and Colin was at the meeting in Kikori, staying with Lewis and Dulcie Parker, whose mission station was near the airstrip, built in swamp country.

A message came to them from the government station, located on the other side of the airstrip, notifying them that a man had been shot in the face at point blank range by a 12-gauge shotgun. He had been caught being amorous with another man's wife and the husband had taken revenge by virtually blowing the offender's face apart.

The damage was too horrific to be handled at the local clinic, so the request was to transport the wounded man to Port Moresby. Colin agreed to do so, even though it was 9 pm and a pitch-black night. He suggested that Lewis, a fellow pilot, accompany him so he might gain more experience in night flying.

After removing all seats in the *Andrew Stewart* except those of the pilot and co-pilot, the semi-conscious patient, brought by doctor-boys on a litter, was loaded into the plane, made as comfortable as possible on the floor and secured with seat belts.

Colin and Lewis prayed over the moaning patient and prepared for takeoff, notifying Port Moresby that they were about to take off with a seriously injured patient on board and requesting that an ambulance be on site for their arrival.

Lantern carriers had lined the edge and across the end of the runway to give direction and light. The whole airstrip was covered in metal Marsden matting that allowed aircraft to land on boggy fields. Obviously this was a leftover from World War II. As a plane landed or took off, it would set up a loud rattling sound as it moved over the metal plates.

The lightly loaded aeroplane lifted quickly above the rattling plates and commenced climbing into the black night sky. Immediately, Colin was dependent on instrument flying and once his designated elevation

Night Flight

had been achieved, set course for Port Moresby, expecting good weather for the flight.

It was a beautiful night for flying as they flew down the coast of Papua, but ahead they saw evidence of a huge storm, indicated by flashes of lightning in the clouds. They would have to fly through the storm to reach their destination.

They soon entered the cloud and hit the turbulence. Sucked high into the air by the up-draught, then plunging earthward by the down-draught, Colin battled with the controls to keep the little plane level. The patient was moaning and crying out in fear throughout the turbulence, it being his first flight. Some 20 minutes later, they popped out of the storm into welcoming smooth air once more.

Ahead could be seen the glow from the lights of Port Moresby. Colin advised Traffic Control of their approach and questioned whether an ambulance had been arranged. He was assured the ambulance was already waiting on the tarmac.

Police and ambulance officers give Lew Parker and Colin a hand in off-loading a shotgun victim. The emergency flight was made at night through stormy weather from Kikori to Port Moresby.

Winchee

The landing was without incident and Colin taxied to the waiting ambulance into which the patient was transferred, then rushed off for immediate surgery. Unknown to the two missionary pilots, the media had been advised of the flight and were on hand to take photos and record the happening for the local newspaper. It was good public relations for the Seventh-day Adventist Church in Papua New Guinea.

Years later, Colin, then president of the Papua New Guinea Union Mission, attended the Papuan Gulf campmeeting and was introduced to a man with a badly scarred face. This was the patient he and Lewis had flown to Port Moresby on that fateful night. The injured man was so impressed with the care provided that, on release from hospital in Port Moresby, he returned to Kikori where he began an association with the local Adventists and had become a baptised church member.

God has a thousand ways to bring about His eternal purposes.

Kikori airstrip was a vital centre for the mission's aviation program throughout the Papuan Gulf and Western Districts of Papua New Guinea. The mission's headquarters can be seen at the top of the picture.

Heroines of Mission

While life for expatriate male missionaries was often exciting, frequently challenging but always busy, the same was not true of their female counterparts. They were always busy and mission life was frequently challenging—but in a different way. Life was usually more dangerous than exciting.

The wife of a missionary on a remote mission station, whether expatriate or national, was often lonely. The husband would be responsible for a large geographical territory and would often be away for weeks at a time, leaving his wife to care for the family needs, including supervising the children's education, as well as overseeing the operation of the mission station. If a nurse, all manner of medical issues and emergencies had to be cared for. Expatriate wives would sometimes go for weeks, months or even a year without seeing another white female. Mail was irregular and essential food supplies were sometimes hard to obtain.

It was little different for national workers' wives. They, too, were often from outside New Guinea and, when placed in a mission outpost, struggled to feed their families until they established their own gardens. Their husbands were also away from home a great deal and were more at risk of being attacked or killed than their expatriate counterparts. This brought a degree of apprehension into the lives of their wives. The uncertainty often seemed worse during the night hours.

Missionary families associated with administration, hospital or educational institutions generally had the advantage of association with other expatriates. Loneliness was less of a problem. Yet there were still dangers to be faced.

A white woman could be said to be safer on an outpost mission station than one living in an urban area where crime was more common. Camp meetings or administrative committee meetings often took their husbands away, at which time even married women were subject to the possibility of attacks from nationals with evil intent. This was particularly true for single expatriate women.

Winchee

Security fences were not the complete answer to New Guinea's crime problem. Torrential rain on wet nights deadens sounds, giving would-be intruders the opportunity to cut through the fence and rob staff housing or carry out other nefarious intents.

As the move from tribal villages to urban dwelling took place, high unemployment increased the crime rate. It was a mounting problem in Papua New Guinea, causing stress to all heroines who have taken their part in sharing the gospel with the inhabitants of this wonderful country.

Another Perspective:

Colin's visits to our home were like a breath of fresh air. Whether it was a scheduled stop when he joined in meetings, deliveries of supplies or personnel, a forced delay because the weather conditions had become too bad to fly, or maybe his permitted hours of flying were up—whatever reason Colin buzzed us to let us know he was landing on the airstrip, the excitement in the family was huge.

We lived in an age of no telephones, a crackly battery radio to try to pick up world news, mail twice a week if we were lucky, and trips to Mt Hagen for shopping every three months.

It was the era when I finally had all three children on correspondence lessons and we listened with some difficulty to the reports of President Kennedy being shot and of man's first landing on the moon. It was back in the days of "telegrams" that took forever to arrive at the nearest government office and we could collect them at the same time as we collected any mail.

So when Pastor Winch arrived the children were very excited. Colin was always a breath of fresh air!

—*Marie Williams, mission director's wife*

Mechanical Difficulties

Tari is located in a valley in the Southern Highlands at an elevation of approximately 5400 feet (1600 metres) and is serviced by a commercial airstrip. District Director Alwyn Galway asked Colin to fly supplies to Komo Mananda, a landing strip 10 minutes by air from Tari. Hiking time would have been two days with a considerable quantity of supplies necessary for the patrol. Colin was happy to assist, knowing this would involve three flights shuttling the goods to a short landing strip that could be dangerous in windy conditions.

With the first load tightly secured and a national pastor in the co-pilot's seat of the Cessna 180, Colin took off from Tari and made a successful landing at Komo Mananda, where the cargo was unloaded. He then returned to Tari and successfully repeated the procedure.

The Tari Airport has a long runway, with a windsock at each end and one in the middle. Often these three windsocks can be blowing in different directions, making landing a matter of guesswork.

As Colin made the approach after his second load, he noted that he would be landing in a crosswind but would run into a headwind at the other end of the runway. He was comfortable with the situation and landed on one wheel to counteract the wind. It was a classic crosswind touch down and Colin congratulated himself, hoping Alwyn Galway had seen it.

Without warning, a strong gusting tailwind hit the tail of the aeroplane, causing the nose of the plane to pitch down, while the tail rose alarmingly. Colin pulled back on the control column to rectify the situation but it jammed. No matter how hard he pulled, it would not budge. He saw gravel rushing past the nose. At any moment, the propeller would strike the surface of the runway and the plane would

Mechanical Difficulties

flip onto its back. He was facing a certain crash.

"God, help me!" he cried.

All of a sudden the tail was pushed down as if some giant hand had put weight on it. He was thrown forward in his harness. Shaking with fear, he yanked at the control column, trying to free it without success. It was still jammed! Eventually he taxied to the parking bay, killed the motor and sat in the cockpit, trembling. It had been the closest he had ever been to crashing a plane.

Alwyn walked around and opened the plane door. Seeing Colin's white face he asked, "What's wrong with you, Winchee?"

"Didn't you see what just happened back there?" Colin responded.

"No! I was reading and didn't see anything."

"Try this control column!" suggested the pilot.

It remained jammed against Alwyn's attempt.

A search revealed that a small piece of fibreglass had come loose and had jammed the elevator, just as the plane touched down. Fortunately, this did not happen at Komo Mananda. Such a little thing—but what frightening consequences if God had not intervened!

* * *

On another occasion, Colin, Elwyn Raethel and a friend of the Raethel family known as Aunty Doris had visited Pastor Paul Piari who was pioneering the work at Kiunga. They taxied to the end of the grass airstrip about to make their return flight to Mt Hagen.

As Colin turned 180 degrees to position the plane for takeoff, they heard a loud bang in the tail section. It was immediately evident that a rudder spring had broken. These light planes were fitted with two opposing rudder springs that hold the rudder in the straight-ahead position. But now the one good spring was holding the rudder hard to one side making it difficult to get the plane to track in a straight line.

Colin taxied slowly back to their starting point and by radio advised the Department of Civil Aviation and mission headquarters of their predicament.

They explained their problem to Pastor Paul and he readily agreed to share his humble home with them for the night. The house was built of bush materials and privacy was minimal.

Winchee

Aunty Doris viewed the circumstances and the house with apprehension. She had lived through the pioneering days of Dora Creek but had never lived in a building as insecure as this one. She had learned that day that there were cannibals in the bush—perhaps not far away. They showed her the only spare room in the house and told her it was hers. Colin and Elwyn slept on the verandah just outside her room. It was an uneventful night but a fitful sleep.

With no replacement spring available by the third day, Colin decided it was time for action. After several practice runs on the airstrip, and noting the good weather, he decided to take off for Mt Hagen. Between the two men they were able to hold the plane on course by maintaining pressure on the rudder pedal. The two-hour flight proved uneventful and Aunty Doris declared the experience to be the highlight of her trip to New Guinea.

Lining up on final approach to land at Kiunga in the Western Gulf. As they prepared for takeoff, it was found that one of the rudder springs had broken and fallen off. There were no aircraft maintenance facilities at Kiunga.

They Heralded the King

"The King's Heralds are coming!" Word spread quickly from mission station to mission station, from village to village. Excitement mounted.

The music produced by the King's Heralds had won the hearts of parents and children alike throughout the Solomon Islands. Their songs were sung, often in four-part harmony, by toddlers playing on the sandy beaches or splashing in the waters of the lagoons. King's Herald songs indelibly recorded in their minds, adults formed quartets singing in harmony difficult to differentiate from that of the King's Heralds themselves.

Now Solomon Islanders were to have the opportunity to see, touch and hear their heroes of gospel music.

Their first visit took place during Colin and Melva's first year of mission service. The Adventists at Kukudu determined to give the King's Heralds a traditional welcome, dressed as fierce warriors with war paint, sounding war cries, wielding war implements and performing war dances. They had spent weeks getting it choreographed. As the *Varivato* arrived with the long-awaited guests on board, they were greeted by an intimidating spectacle.

This "welcome" spectacle over, everyone wanted to shake hands with the celebrities. The King's Heralds were humble men and were overwhelmed by the warmth of the welcome and the vast numbers who had gathered to hear them sing. Nationals had travelled from all over the Western Solomons, some even paddled for two days by canoe.

The *Erovo* (meeting house) was packed to capacity and a hush fell over the audience as the quartet was about to sing. Many of those

Winchee

present had adored the King's Herald's music for years. As the beautiful harmonies rang out, there was thunderous applause that seemed to go on forever. Colin observed that the audience sat open-mouthed in awe and deep respect as song after song added to the rapturous atmosphere.

No doubt the visitors retired to their beds that night with a great sense of satisfaction. But they were not to get a good sleep. Rats saw to that!

Colin and Melva occupied the most commodious house on the Kukudu Mission Station and were happy to provide accommodation for the honoured guests. Having settled them in their rooms, Colin and Melva retired to their bed but were disturbed by a commotion from the visitors' part of the house.

Dressed in his pyjamas, Colin knocked on one of the doors to hear a very agitated, "Come in!"

Opening the door, he saw the two occupants standing on their beds,

The King's Heralds climbed into a Karamul village house to see "how the other half lives" during a singing tour throughout Papua New Guinea and the Solomon Islands. Colin provided the air transport.

They Heralded the King

peering down at a large Solomon Island rodent. The earlier welcome by the warriors had not daunted them—but the intrusion of this rodent sure did.

* * *

The second tour by the King's Heralds took place early in 1973. Colin met them at Port Moresby and flew them in the *J L Tucker* to their various appointments throughout Papua New Guinea. Before departure, each member was weighed with their luggage. This was standard procedure for all passenger flights as there were legal load limits in place and Colin rigidly adhered to these limits. A second plane was used to transport their sound equipment.

As with all visitors, the King's Heralds marvelled at the scenes laid out below them. Huge rivers with their wide deltas, towering jagged mountains with sheer cliff faces, waterfalls cascading into tropical forests, fertile valleys contrasted with arid rain-shadowed plains. The men seated in the back of the plane had a better view than the passenger in the front who looked out over the wing.

They soon recognised the skill involved in flying a small plane in such a land of contrasts but felt secure with Colin as their "Captain," knowing that before takeoff he would always commit all involved into the care of a loving God.

The King's Heralds experienced first-hand the difficulty of fulfilling all appointments. Clouded-in mountains often made flying hazardous and the search for a way over the mountain passes sometimes proved futile.

Such was the case when an attempt was made to meet an appointment at Kabiufa. Hundreds of the local people had gathered in this Eastern Highland centre in anticipation of hearing the songs they knew so well from the singers themselves.

The weather was adverse and Colin flew back and forth, trying to find a safe hole or break in the clouds. Proximity to the jagged rocks peeping through the clouds was a foreboding sight to those unaccustomed to such conditions. Finally, the attempt had to be aborted and one can only imagine the disappointment of those assembled.

Winchee

* * *

But there were more successful flights than disappointing ones. Jim McClintock (King's Heralds bass, 1962–1977) recalled landing at the crushed coral airstrip at Emirau. At the time of the visit by the King's Heralds, the Seventh-day Adventist mission planes were the only ones using it. The trees were growing back but there was sufficient clearing for the mission planes to land.

The Adventist members had marked out a place for the group to stand. A couple of primitively dressed and adorned nationals performed their cannibalistic war dances, providing an atmosphere of realism from their pre-Christian past, before singing of a different nature could be heard coming from among the trees. Quite a large group came marching and singing until they were all in front of the King's Heralds, demonstrating the transformation brought about by the gospel. It was an emotional experience that brought tears to the eyes of the visitors.

The three-hour trip to Mussau had to be made by sea as there was

Colin prepares to use bathroom scales to weigh his passengers before departing Port Moresby for the group's singing tour.

They Heralded the King

no landing strip on Mussau. The King's Heralds boarded the *Malalagi* but soon three of them suffered from seasickness. Being used to the sea, Jerry Patton made light of his fellow singers' predicament, even describing what each had eaten that morning as they lost their breakfast overboard.

On landing at Boliu, still feeling unwell but happy to be on dry land, the singers faced a sea of a different nature—a sea of expectant faces. The Mussau people loved singing and the King's Heralds were their heroes. Still others had crossed the sea from Emirau to be present. So big was the crowd that the performance had to be shifted from the school auditorium to the sports ground.

A fabulous evening of gospel music was enjoyed by all. The local people sang in their beautiful harmony to the King's Heralds, who responded by singing to the crowd. Long into the evening, the music wafted on the tropical breezes. There were just a few hours left for the King's Heralds to snatch a little sleep before boarding the *Malalagi* for their return to Emirau.

Colin affirmed that the visit of the King's Heralds did more to bring together the church in the Western Solomons than anything he had ever known.

Another Perspective:

I had only been in the King's Heralds four months when, on Christmas Day, 1972, we headed out for a seven-week tour of the South Pacific. After a wonderful time in New Zealand and Australia, "Captain Colin" carefully weighed each of us and our hand-carried bags, loaded us into a six-seat Piper Aztec, and headed out for mysterious places unknown by this group of "city boys."

I'll never forget the sight of the little grass airstrip coming up at us as we landed in the Highlands of New Guinea. Soon we realised that the quartet's music and the word of God as presented by Pastor Winch were falling on receptive ears.

One thing that particularly impressed us about Pastor Winch was the wonderful way he preached to these folk in Pidgin English. I found it to be a language that was beautiful in its simplicity. The word for "God" struck me as particularly descriptive—"Big Man walk along top." Our quartet even sang a song in Pidgin, of which I still remember the first couple of lines: "One time. One time, me walk one time Jesus. Big fella, liklik fella, Jesus laikim you."

Pastor Winch's care in safely piloting us from one tiny island to the next will be forever etched in my memory. Only in heaven will the full extent of his loving ministry to these folk be known.

—*John Ramsey, King's Heralds, First Tenor, 1971–82*

Earthquake

For anyone who has lived in Papua New Guinea, the name "Rabaul" will inevitably be associated with earthquakes. It is a town in the East New Britain province of Papua New Guinea with a beautiful circular harbour but located in close proximity to active volcanoes. Over the years, volcanic activity and earthquakes have been a constant concern. A series of major earthquakes occurred in 1971, followed by a destructive tsunami. The Winch family was resident in Rabaul at the time.

Late in July, Colin had flown Pastor Gordon Lee and Ted Jones to Kieta in Bougainville, where they parked the plane and were picked up by the local mission president and taken to meetings in Rhumba where there was a central boarding school.

Pastor Lee preached the evening sermon and everyone retired to their beds. In the middle of the night, the houses began to rattle and shake. Being built on stilts, they even swayed as a strong earthquake rippled through the area. Even though the epicentre was some 150 nautical miles (280 kilometres) away in the sea south of Rabaul, the result was that fridge doors burst open with the contents spilling out onto the floors and books were dislodged from shelves, adding to the chaos.

Without fuss, the visitors climbed out of bed and returned the spilled food to the fridge but left the books in a heap on the floor until the morning. They returned to their beds and went to sleep. It was just another earthquake!

The next morning—July 26, 1971—the three men returned to Kieta where Colin went through the usual routine of carefully checking the plane prior to takeoff. Following a prayer for protection, the engines roared into life and they commenced their 90-minute flight to Rabaul.

As they flew over the ocean, a strange sight appeared below. It was as if someone had dropped a huge rock into the ocean, causing rippling waves going out in all directions. Gordon Lee described it as similar to what happens when someone pulls the plug on a bath full of water, only this vortex was on a much grander scale.

Winchee

Colin reported the sight to Flight Service Control, to be informed, "You're right over the epicentre of an 8.7 earthquake."

Such a strong earthquake would create a tsunami. As Colin circled the area viewing the phenomenon, a request came through, asking him to divert to Nissan Island, a low-lying inhabited atoll with which radio contact had been lost. It was feared that the island might have been totally destroyed by the tsunami.

Responding to the request, Colin flew low over Nissan Island to find that all was well, except that the radio masts were down. Hence no radio contact.

When the radio was switched to Rabaul Airport Control, Colin was instructed to "Land short!" as a major section of the Rabaul runway had been cracked by the earthquake.

When the *J L Tucker* safely landed in Rabaul, the Winch children excitedly surrounded their father, all wanting to talk at the same time about the tsunami.

The water level in the Simpson Harbour rose, then fell about 11 feet

The Winch family at Rabaul in 1972: (back row, left to right) Kerry, Melva, Colin, Carol; (front row, left to right) Chris, Nerolie.

Earthquake

(3.5 metres) leaving the harbour bed dry. Excitedly, the children rushed down to view the phenomenon only to be told by a national policeman, "Go back! Go back! Water he come!"

Soon the water came rushing back, gathering speed as it flooded into the town, rushing through doors and windows on its path of destruction. The waves washed back and forth like water in a gold mining pan. The Winch children saw a Volkswagen car floating in the water while tethered to a verandah post.

Mango Avenue was the town's main road, and contained the supermarkets and the two main stores. Most of their goods and produce were thrown from the shelves by the quake, then inundated by water from the tsunami. Loss for some is gain for others and the residents of Rabaul benefited from cheap prices for some time.

Some of the town's children thought Christmas had come in July when they picked up cans of soft drink and food that had been washed from stores and carried down the roads. They also rejoiced in the two weeks free from classes as their classrooms had been damaged and the strong aftershocks were considered life-threatening should children be trapped in already-damaged classrooms.

With aftershocks occurring on a minute-by-minute basis, many of the Chinese residents and shopkeepers simply fled the town.

The Winch children became amateur seismologists, claiming they could tell when a shake was coming. Colin was doubtful until they led him outside and, before long, said, "Dad! It is coming. We can hear it!" Sure enough, there was a drumming noise from the water tanks as the quake approached.

The children also claimed to be able to see the quake approaching. In even greater doubt, Colin was taken out into the middle of a straight road, where they all waited. "There! Look!" he was told.

"I can't see anything!" Colin responded.

"Look down the road, Dad!"

Colin then saw the road rising and falling in a ripple effect as the quake progressed toward them and was felt underfoot.

As a result of the series of earthquakes, many of the roads were badly damaged.

Approximately 12 miles (19 kilometres) from Rabaul, the staff houses

Winchee

at Sonoma College, built on stilts, had to be braced by galvanised pipe stays on all four corners. The Adventist harbour village of Matapit suddenly found it was given a large beach as the quake forced the earth upward.

The Winch family thanked the Lord for their safekeeping in such dangerous but exciting times and the memory of their experience at Rabaul remains a highlight in the children's minds.

A Critical Omission

In anticipation of Papua New Guinea being granted independence, the Seventh-day Adventist Church voted in 1972 to realign the island Union Missions. All of New Guinea's offshore islands became part of the Papua New Guinea Union Mission and the balance of the former Bismark–Solomons Union Mission became the Western Pacific Union Mission, including the New Hebrides (now Vanuatu), Gilbert and Ellice Islands (Kiribati and Tuvalu) and New Caledonia.

Rabaul being located in Papua New Guinea, it became necessary to re-locate the headquarters for the newly formed Western Pacific Union Mission. These were built at Honiara, the seat of the High Commissioner for the Western Pacific.

Colin recalls the day he and Gordon Lee, president of the Union Mission, walked over the land determining where buildings should be located. A high flood-free elevated point overlooking the Lunga River was chosen.

One day, Pastor Lee was on a commercial flight, seated alongside a businessman looking to expand his earth-moving business into the Solomon Islands. He was searching for a site on which to locate his heavy equipment.

Pastor Lee saw it as a God-given opportunity. He offered to have the equipment on mission land on the condition that the church could use the bulldozer for a couple of weeks. Prior to working for the church, he had worked with heavy earth-moving equipment.

A deal was struck and the levelling of building sites was done for only the cost of fuel to the church.

The Winch family moved to Honiara in 1973, the first expatriate family of the Western Pacific Union Mission staff to do so. Colin continued his work as Union Pilot, Youth and Health Director.

Not only was the family happy in their new location and comfortable home, but Colin loved working with young people and the challenge of oversight of Atoifi Hospital. The various medical

Winchee

clinics also profited from his nursing training. Flying also took on a new dimension as much of his work involved long flights across oceans and dealing with customs, health and immigration authorities of island nations.

* * *

On one occasion, Colin and Max Miller, the Education and Temperance Director of the Western Pacific Union mission, had completed an itinerary of the New Hebrides Mission and were about to fly from Santo to church headquarters in Honiara. Seeing that the plane was lightly loaded, Colin decided to fill all available tanks with aviation fuel as it was cheaper in Santo than in Honiara. The 160 gallons (600 litres) involved would achieve a considerable saving.

While the tanks were being filled, Colin completed the paperwork required for the international flight. Commercial pilots have this work done for them, but not pilots of private flights. Passenger manifest, cargo manifest and a host of other documentation had to be completed.

Western Pacific Union Mission Committee, including Colin (third row, left), meeting at Betikama High School, circa 1975.

A Critical Omission

He then commenced checking the plane for the three-hour flight across the Coral Sea to Honiara.

He carefully checked that the refuelling vehicle had not damaged the external skin of the plane and was in the process of making these checks when the person who had refuelled the plane called for him to sign for the fuel. On return, he failed to check the petrol cap on the outboard starboard wing. The person refuelling the plane would normally clamp the cap shut but it was Colin's responsibility to make doubly sure this was done.

Having satisfactorily completed all the paperwork, Colin took off on a cloudy morning, climbed to 8500 feet (2500 metres) to clear Mt Tabwemasana on the western side of the island, then set a direct course for Honiara. Visibility was good over the Coral Sea and, not being under time pressure, Colin throttled back the engines to achieve the most economical flight, setting the plane on autopilot. A few moments before reaching the critical half-way point, Colin looked out to starboard and noticed that the petrol cap on the starboard tip tank was venting. Fuel was being sucked out of the tank!

He had two choices: keep going to Honiara or return to Santo.

Colin weighed up the alternatives. He did not like the idea of flying over the Santo mountains with a fuel problem. On the other hand, a forced landing into the Coral Sea also lacked appeal.

He decided to keep going, as Honiara had better firefighting equipment than Santo, even though the flight time was the same. He decided to switch both engines on to the venting tank to use up the remaining fuel quickly and minimise the loss. This could have two consequences. The plane could become unbalanced and, should the tank be sucked dry, there was a risk of engine failure. Switching to the starboard tank, Colin carefully monitored the fuel-pressure gauge.

Max had also noted the venting and drew Colin's attention to it. He tended to be a nervous flyer, so Colin assured him everything was under control. Colin estimated that, having filled all tanks in Santo, there should be a reserve of approximately five hours flying time on landing in Honiara. The secret to successfully dealing with the situation was when to switch from the venting tank to the tanks on the port wing. When Colin estimated there might be half an hour's fuel left in

Winchee

the venting tank, he switched one of the engines to a full tank on the port wing while still carefully monitoring the fuel pressure gauge on the venting tank. As soon as the pressure began to drop, the second engine was switched over to a full starboard tank.

Without further drama, the flight was completed and they landed safely in Honiara.

But Colin castigated himself for his carelessness. He mulled over how he failed to make the appropriate check. Time and again, he had stressed to other mission pilots not to allow themselves to be distracted when making pre-flight checks, now he had broken his own rule. Had he not filled all tanks at Santo, the flight might have had a different ending.

Prayers of thankfulness ascended to God that night.

A Presidential Visit

Life for Bryan and Dawn Ball took a new twist when Bryan was elected president of the South Pacific Division. Born in England, Bryan had become a well-respected academic and writer. Having served as the head of Biblical Studies at Newbold College (England), Dr Ball had been president of Avondale College in Cooranbong (Australia) when his election as president changed the direction of his life.

In 1991, Dawn accompanied Bryan on one of his many visits to the Solomon Islands and Papua New Guinea and Colin happily flew them from appointment to appointment. Sadly, just before the Ball's arrival, Colin had returned to Australia to attend his mother's funeral. But he hastened back to Honiara where he met up with Bryan and Dawn.

Having a reputation as a careful, praying pilot, Colin demonstrated this habit each day as he prepared the plane for flight. This gave assurance to Bryan and Dawn that—between God and Colin—they were in good hands.

As with many visitors to the Pacific islands, Bryan and Dawn quickly noted the difference Christianity had made to the local people. Hostility has been replaced by friendliness; smiling, radiant faces had replaced surly countenances.

Though not expecting the highways of an Australian city, Bryan and Dawn were nonetheless surprised by the transport that awaited them as they flew in to Atoifi. They were met at the airstrip by a tractor towing a specially-decorated trailer on which two armchairs were mounted.

Atoifi is a wet place receiving heavy rainfall. Consequently the steep track up to the hospital compound was both muddy and deeply rutted. With children running alongside the trailer, the visiting dignitaries hung on tightly as the trailer rocked and rolled its way to the mission compound.

In Gizo, capital of the Western Province of the Solomon Islands, the local Adventists wished to give Dr and Mrs Ball a traditional welcome so Bryan and Dawn were to be transported by 40 warriors paddling a decorated native canoe. They were taken via Kennedy Island, named after John F Kennedy, who had been washed ashore after a naval battle during World War II. The ocean was choppy not making for an easy crossing, especially for Dawn. But she was stoic in the face of these new experiences.

On arrival, they were immediately confronted by swarms of highly decorated, half-naked "warriors" armed to the teeth with spears and bows and arrows, in mock defence of their island. Aware that it was a "mock up" Bryan could not help thinking, "If this is a welcome, what would an 'unwelcome' be like?" Dawn coped well with it all until at a later meeting the visitors were announced as "Dr and Lady Ball." The sea had not made her squirm but that introduction surely did.

Bryan was keen to learn firsthand about the reports of devil possession in pre-Christian times. Passing a beach while walking with a local pastor, Bryan was told that a national had picked up a fallen coconut on that very beach and it turned in his hand into the leering face of a devil. Other pastors confirmed similar incidents. Foreign to the Western-educated mind, this vindicated the tremendous transformation from fear to joy that the gospel had wrought in the lives of these simple-living people.

* * *

A highlight of the trip for Bryan was a visit to Mussau. He had read of the miraculous conversion of its people and wished to see the transformation for himself. There is no airstrip on Mussau, so, having flown to a neighbouring island, the crossing to Mussau had to be by canoe.

The 30-minute trip proved eventful when a sudden tropical storm broke overhead. The paddlers quickly covered their guests with tarpaulins and the rest of the crossing was spent in total darkness, listening to the rain beating on the tarpaulins.

On arrival, the rain had stopped and there was time for a quick lunch before entering the large church for the main meeting. Electricity on Mussau is supplied by generators, so the meeting was held in the afternoon to avoid their use.

While visiting the island, Bryan and Dawn were guests of one of the local workers for the night. A special "shower" had been erected in the garden, consisting of plastic sheeting wrapped around four bush poles. The covering hid everything from neck to knees, depending on how tall one was.

Their charming hosts could speak quite good English and gave them a wonderful supper by the light of an oil lamp. But sleep was hard to come by due to unaccustomed noises for much of the night caused by rats scurrying about and climbing into the thatched roof.

The local people were mindful of the homeland of their guests. Colin flew them to New Georgia where they were taken by boat for a brief ride on Viru Harbour. The calm waters had been decorated with little islands of floating hyacinth, all bearing English names.

Throughout their tour, the Balls were entertained by musical renditions from children, adult quartets and even the famous Solomon Island bamboo band, which was later to play at a General Conference session.

Reporting the visit to New Georgia, Bryan wrote, "All this had taken place in the full afternoon sun, and we were hot, but the ingenuity of the local people had not yet been exhausted. We were taken to the home of one of the island leaders and asked if we would like a shower.

"Someone had rigged up a shower cubicle, Western-style, in an outhouse, clearly with some difficulty, since there was little water pressure to make a shower work! It was actually a hose-pipe dangling from a beam that provided a thin trickle of cold water when turned on. One had to stand directly underneath on a board to get the benefit, and the whole thing was next to an open latrine. I went first and then Dawn, while a group of local ladies sat around on the ground outside, waiting in case we needed any help and to make sure we enjoyed ourselves.

"We spent that night, well-showered and very well fed local-style, in a native hut with open windows, and in the morning after breakfast ,we all went down to the church for a farewell meeting."

Bryan and Dawn gave thanks to God for safe travel and the opportunity to witness firsthand the transforming power of the gospel. Asked about Colin's piloting skills, Dr Ball responded with true English conservatism, "Colin is an excellent pilot!"

Another Perspective:

The first and most vivid experience that I recall was Colin's ability to tell stories to the Kukudu school children gathered in the Kukudu *Erovo* (meeting house) one evening. I can still hear the oohs and ahs and eees of the children as Colin related his first attempts to fly an aeroplane. Without doubt, it was one of the best stories told so beautifully and impressively in the Pidgin language. They were literally out of their seats with such excitement.

Colin is a storyteller without peer in my estimation. I'm sure the story wouldn't be half so hilarious in English and I was impressed with his ability to express himself in Pidgin. I never could master the Pidgin language to that extent.

—*Bert Godfrey, retired mission president*

"Nauru! To the right?"

In 1970, the Bismark–Solomons Union Mission (BSUM) was presented with a brand new Piper Aztec twin-engine aeroplane. Pastor John Lee, who had been Youth Director for the BSUM, had promoted Adventist Aviation, including contacting the Quiet Hour radio and television program in the United States appealing for financial help. After many negotiations, this ministry offered to purchase the plane for the BSUM. On arrival, the aeroplane was dedicated in Rabaul and named the *J L Tucker* after the originator of The Quiet Hour program.

This was a God-send to the BSUM but they had no-one qualified to fly it. As Colin was the fulltime pilot for the Coral Sea Union Mission (CSUM) and had previous experience flying Piper Aztec aeroplanes, he was invited to add the responsibility of flying for the BSUM to his work for the CSUM. This meant increased time away from home but as they were then located in Lae where the children were able to attend school, Melva was able to obtain paid employment.

After time with this arrangement, because the aeroplane belonged to the BSUM, the new president Pastor Gordon Lee decided he needed to have the plane based in Rabaul, so called Colin to Rabaul as the Youth and Health Director of the BSUM. The Winch family were happy to return to the Union of their first appointment in mission service.

The *J L Tucker* was used in long-range trans-ocean flying to New Caledonia, the New Hebrides (now Vanuatu), Nauru, the Gilbert (Kiribati) and Ellice (Tuvalu) Islands, throughout the Solomon Island missions and on numerous occasions to Fiji transporting students to and from Fulton College. The flight to Fiji would take seven hours—to the Gilberts, seven hours via Nauru. Colin found this to be interesting flying.

Winchee

* * *

A flight north to Tarawa, capital of the Gilberts, via Nauru was planned as the recently-appointed Pastor Lee wished to pay a visit, together with Max Miller and Ted Jones, some of his departmental leaders. Colin, the pilot, would also represent the Youth and Health Departments. The flight to Nauru would take four-and-a-half hours with full fuel. The endurance of the plane was five-and-a-half hours, but six-and-a-half hours if Colin set the engines for long-range flying. This he did. This would give several hours buffer with fuel in reserve. Months earlier, six drums of aviation fuel had been ordered from Australia to be shipped to Nauru and notification was received that these had arrived.

On takeoff, the plane was carrying maximum legal weight and was taken to the 7000-foot (about 2100-metres) cruising height on course for Nauru, dependent for the accuracy of their flight on Radio Direction Finding Beacons at Honiara and Nauru. However, there would be several hours when they would be out of range of either beacon.

Colin tracked out for around 160 miles (250 kilometres) on the

The new Piper Aztec's first flight to Nauru from Honiara.

"Nauru! To the right?"

Honiara beacon before losing contact. After flying for another 90 minutes in beautiful weather with a glistening sea below, the Nauru Non-Directional Beacon began to show on the instrument panel of the Aztec and the needles on the radio compasses swung to indicate Nauru was straight ahead.

After about an hour more of flying, both Gordon and Colin noticed that the needles were beginning to turn slowly to the right, indicating—if they were to be believed—that Nauru was coming past them on the right.

"Winchee! Look at those needles! We are off course! Nauru is out on our right-hand side!" exclaimed Gordon.

"It can't be!" replied Colin. "We haven't been in the air long enough yet!"

After another 20 minutes of flying, the needles were pointing at right angles to the direction in which they were going. Still later, they were pointing slightly behind, indicating that the aeroplane was now well past Nauru.

Nauru is only a tiny island and not easy to see as the highest point on the island is only about 60 feet (18 metres) above sea level. Still, because of the time that had elapsed since departure, Colin was certain that they had not yet reached Nauru.

"Are you sure, Winchee? Shouldn't we turn and follow the direction of the compass needles?" questioned Gordon, with consternation in his voice.

"I am sure Nauru is dead ahead, Gordon. We have not been flying long enough to reach the island. We will keep going on our present course," responded Colin.

"You'd better be right!" muttered Gordon as he looked out over the expanse of water below. He knew the plane was fitted with a six-man inflatable life raft, life jackets for all on board, and survival rations including plenty of water, in case of a ditching. But the possibility was not one he looked forward to!

Colin was convinced there was something faulty with the two radio compasses in the aeroplane, even though both were indicating Nauru was now behind them to the right. Thirty minutes more of flying and in the distance they could see a little cloud, indicating there was land ahead.

Winchee

"I'm sure Nauru is under that cloud!" Colin told his passengers.

True to his word, as they neared the cloud, the little island of Nauru appeared. Suddenly, the two radio compasses swung back and pointed dead ahead. Everyone breathed a sigh of relief and tension within the plane dispersed as they made a safe landing on the paved airstrip.

Colin paid a visit to the control tower to ask what had happened. The officer apologised, saying that they had omitted to turn the beacon on until shortly before Colin landed.

The group spent the night at the local hotel and met with the Adventists who were working at the phosphate mine on Nauru. They then flew on to the Gilberts.

Much later, on returning from the trip, Colin had an aircraft radio technician check the radio compasses in the Aztec. He found that whoever had originally fitted them had done so incorrectly. Both radio compasses were working off one sense antenna instead of each having their individual antenna. This had caused the compasses to read incorrectly and, had Colin not chosen to ignore them, could have resulted in a major catastrophe.

* * *

The fuel dump at Nauru was extremely important because, even with long-range fuel tanks fitted to the aeroplane, there was not enough fuel to have the safe reserves required for their destinations. Forty-four gallon (160-litre) drums of aviation fuel—Avgas—were continually being shipped to Nauru.

On one flight, Colin arrived at Nauru to find that the pilot of an itinerate aircraft had stolen all the stored fuel. This was a real challenge!

There was sufficient Avgas in the Aztec to get from Nauru to Tarawa, but not enough for the required reserves. In desperation, it was decided to up-load regular automobile fuel into separate tanks of the aeroplane but not to use it unless it was absolutely necessary. In that way the flight to Tarawa was achieved, the fuel emptied—much to the delight of the local mission president—and the tanks re-filled with Avgas.

God had His hand over all these matters and Colin saw evidence on a daily basis of His leading, protection and blessings.

Living With the Unexpected

The Winch family had driven in their Toyota Corolla station wagon to the markets in Honiara and had done their fruit and vegetable shopping in the native market.

On completion of this task, they all had the treat of a soft-serve ice-cream. Colin noticed that the ice cream tasted a little sour and concluded it was just going off. He continued to eat his, as did Melva, Kerry, Nerolie and Chris. But Carol was having difficulty with hers.

As they drove across the one-way bridge crossing the small river near the Honiara township, she complained that her ice-cream was "Yucky." She wasn't eating it and it was starting to drip onto the car seat.

In frustration, Colin told her to wind down her window and throw it into the river. She did! But a national man walking in the opposite direction on the pedestrian walkway caught the full impact of the sticky, melting ice-cream in his face.

The children screamed, "Dad! Put your foot down!"

Colin wanted to stop but he was in the middle of a one-way bridge and there were cars following behind and cars in front waiting to make the crossing. Colin felt he had to respond to the demands of his giggling children.

Reluctantly, Colin drove away and the aggrieved national soon gave up the chase!

* * *

Another mishap occurred in the Solomon Islands in 1956 when Colin was appointed as superintendent of the Amyes Memorial Hospital

Winchee

and District Director of the Choiseul District. Sailing on the *Varivato*, Colin and Melva took seven hours to make the crossing to Choiseul, then to a beautiful protected harbour at Katalusa village, where they planned to stay for the Sabbath.

On Sabbath morning, Colin went ashore in the dinghy, sending it back with the boat crew to pick up Melva and their handsome little adopted Solomon Island boy, Galo. However, as Melva, with Galo under one arm, went to step aboard the dinghy from the stern of the *Varivato*, the dinghy separated from the mother-ship and Melva and Galo fell into the clear waters of the harbour. Though unscheduled, it was a pleasant Sabbath-morning dip.

Both were totally submerged but fortunately little Galo, still in Melva's arms, came up laughing, thinking it was great fun. He was handed to the embarrassed crew and Melva clambered aboard and went into the cabin to change both herself and Galo into dry clothes before heading ashore to attend Sabbath worship.

* * *

Rurusan, captain of the *Malalagi*, was noted as a great spear fisherman. He and his crew would often go fishing, sometimes in company with Colin. Mussau men were generally clever with their homemade spear guns and were able to descend to incredible depths without breathing apparatus.

On one occasion, Colin was fishing with Rurusan when he saw him dive down the face of a huge coral reef that went to a tremendous depth. Down, down, down he went with loaded speargun in his right hand, propelling himself with his left hand and legs. Eventually he stopped, stabilised himself, took aim, and fired his spear into a cavern.

By this time, he was running low on oxygen and so began to ascend, using his left hand and legs to propel himself to the surface. Shooting up out of the water, he informed Colin he had shot a large groper. Gropers can weigh as much as 88 pounds (40 kilograms) and grow to longer than five feet (1.5 metres).

Filling his lungs with air once more, he again dived to the depths and nosed into the groper's lair. There he struggled to extricate his catch, using his legs as leverage against the entrance of the cavern.

Living With the Unexpected

But the fish was having none of it!

Colin had been watching this whole performance, wondering at the bravery of the man—or was it foolishness? The groper could easily come out of its lair and disembowel him. But Rurusan was determined! If he couldn't get the fish, at least he wanted his spear back.

By this time, he was out of oxygen again and he rapidly ascended, hitting the surface with a roar and gasp for air. He informed Colin the spear had penetrated the skull of the fish. He doubted he would be able to get the fish out but was determined not to lose his sharpened reinforcing-rod homemade spear.

Down he went again, to a depth of at least 60 feet (18 metres).

Again, he put his feet on each side of the entrance of the cavern and pulled and pulled. Eventually the spearhead came out and he returned to the surface, bitterly disappointed he had not succeeded in dragging the groper from the cavern.

He would have gone down again if Colin had agreed to accompany him, feeling sure the two of them could extricate the huge fish. But Colin would have none of it. He knew he was out of his depth.

* * *

When the Winch family was based at Maprik in the Sepik district of Papua New Guinea, they lived on the banks of a shallow river appropriately named the Screw River. It meandered down from the mountains, across the elevated plains, through the hills, bending backwards and forwards like a screw. Heavy rains in the mountains would produce a bore—a mini tidal wave—that would rush down the river within an hour or two, gathering momentum and size as it made its way through the bends.

The roar of the approaching bore could be heard from some distance away, so Colin and Melva would stand by the church, built on an elevated bank adjacent to the river, to watch the increase in the flow of the shallow stream build up until around the bend would come this three- or four-foot (1-metre) wave, rolling logs, timber and debris before it. It was an awesome visual and audible reminder of the power of water, having the effect of temporarily isolating the mission station from the government station on the other side of the river.

Winchee

Colin noted all the timber being swept past, and as there were almost no trees useful for firewood on the mission station, he decided it would be a great idea to lasso some of the logs and manhandle them ashore. Some ropes were prepared and logs snared but the power of the water only dragged those people on the end of the rope into the stream. Valuable ropes were lost.

A better idea was to build a rock jetty diagonally across half of the river. As the water flowed around the curve in the river, it brought most of the debris onto the mission station side, so the jetty could trap some of the logs, thus providing a source of firewood.

Rocks and stones were in plentiful supply in the river itself, so the rock wall was built when the water levels were low. At the next big rainfall, the jetty was put to the test and proved a success. Young nationals would enter the eddying waters and grab the logs being directed toward the shore, hauling them to dry land. The mission station was kept in firewood for the months of the dry season. There were times, however, when the flow of the river was too strong and a national would be washed downstream before being able to scramble to shore again.

Nonetheless, the idea of a jetty was deemed a great success.

Animals in the Family

Animals were often part of the Winch family. Dogs, cats, birds and a possum were all loved and cared for at various times. Kerry was particularly fond of animals and recalls them all being loaded into the plane when the family was transferring from Lae to Rabaul. During the flight, the possum climbed up on Colin's shoulder. Fortunately, the plane was on automatic pilot at the time, so it did not hinder his flying ability.

On returning from one of their furloughs, the family had acquired two guinea pigs. Kerry was determined to take them with her to Honiara, regardless of the warning that these prized pets might be confiscated by quarantine authorities either in Australia or on landing in Honiara.

A zip-up bag became the animals' temporary home and the flight from Sydney to Brisbane proved no problem. But an overnight stopover in Brisbane was the next hurdle. The guinea pigs were smuggled into the hotel room and spent the night in the bath. Kerry plucked some grass to make sure her pets did not starve and duly took them outside in the morning to allow them to run around, feed and toilet.

The flight from Brisbane to Honiara was the next drama. When the authorities were informed of the plan to take guinea pigs on the plane, the family were advised it would not be permitted but were referred to "the man at the gate." This gentleman was pleaded with in appropriate terms but, when he adamantly declined permission, Kerry burst into tears, sobbing uncontrollably.

She was inconsolable. Her precious pets were confiscated and she understood their lives would be taken from them. So great was her grief that "the man at the gate" was almost in tears himself.

Winchee

The door of the plane was about to close when the said gentleman rushed in and strode to Kerry's seat and thrust a box containing the guinea pigs into her arms. "Here! Take these and put them under your seat—and don't let anyone know they're there!" With that, he made a hurried exit from the plane.

On arrival at the airport in Honiara, Colin informed the Solomons' quarantine officer that they were bringing guinea pigs with them.

"Pigs! Pigs!" exclaimed the officer.

"No! *Guinea* Pigs!" replied Colin.

The officer peered into the box at the two multi-coloured guinea pigs. "*Emi no pig! Emi pussycat!*" he said with a puzzled look on his face.

"No!" assured Colin. "They are guinea pigs!"

The still-confused officer waved them through.

Guinea pigs are prolific breeders, so the Winch children sold the offspring to other expatriate children living in Honiara. Unfortunately for the guinea pigs, they were allergic to the DDT sprayed on all expatriate homes to prevent malaria. The Winch children soon lost this source of income.

* * *

Pastor Gordon Lee was given a Coconut Lorikeet by one of the nationals, which he managed to tame and named Rosie. Rosie learned to talk and used to annoy Gordon's daughter, Michella, by constant chattering while she was trying to read. Michella would tell it to "Shut up!" and the bird soon picked up the words, repeating over and over, "Shut up!"

When the newly-built Western Pacific Union Mission headquarters at Honiara were being opened, the Governor-General of the Solomon Islands was one of the guests. He was standing in the family home with his back to Rosie's cage, speaking to family members as Rosie repeated over and over, "Shut up!"

When the Lees left Honiara, they bequeathed Rosie to the Winch family. This colourful tiny terror would fly all around the mission compound during the day but return home at night. The bird knew which office Colin worked in and would fly in the window and sit on his shoulder. If he was on the phone, Rosie would sit on the headpiece, purportedly listening in on the conversation.

Animals in the Family

"Naughty Rosie" struck fear into the hearts of all the Winch children—except Nerolie. Nerolie loved Rosie and Rosie loved Nerolie. At the end of each day, Rosie would tap on the shut door with its beak, demanding entry. Nerolie would open the door and pick up the bird, while the rest of the children scattered to their rooms.

The flooring in the home was of polished timber and could be slippery under certain circumstances. One evening, young Chris was a little slow to take refuge from Rosie. In desperation, he lost traction before skidding down the long hallway toward his parents' bedroom.

Grabbing the opportunity with both claws, Rosie gave chase, half-flying, half-waddling. Chris slammed the door and Rosie crashed into it, unable to stop in time, then proceeded to tap on the shut door, all the time saying, "Naughty Rosie!" "Naughty Rosie!"

At bedtime, Nerolie would share her bed with Rosie. The bird would lie on its back on the pillow with its legs in the air and Nerolie would cover its body with the sheet and the two would sleep together. One can only imagine the smile on Naughty Rosie's face!

Rosie was a Solomon Coconut Lorrikeet, a treasured pet of the Lees and the Winches, visiting Colin in his office.

The Day Nationals Turned White

Colin Winch was transporting a national worker and his family to their parish on Tongoa Island—one of the Vanuatu group of islands to the north of Vila. With him in the co-pilot's seat was his New Zealand friend, Colin Crawford, known to all as "Crawf."

On radioing the appropriate authorities on the island, Colin asked the condition of the airstrip.

"It's good!" he was told. "We mowed it the other day!"

The weather was good and the sky clear as the steep-sided mountain appeared in front of them and, as the airstrip came into view, it almost had a white look about it.

"Expect a bump as we cross the coast," warned Colin.

The wily pilot kept the nose up for some time before allowing the nose-wheel to touch the ground. Either the radio informant had been in a coma for several days or the grass was the "Jack in the Beanstalk" variety.

At the cliff edge, it was ankle-high but grew taller as they progressed along the landing strip. Looking back where the landing had taken place, there were two wheel tracks where the grass had been flattened and the gradual depression in the middle of these tracks where the nose-wheel had been lowered. On either side was a pile of grass seeds harvested by the propeller tips.

As the worker's family disembarked, a queue of would-be passengers had formed.

Inspection done, prayer offered, pre-flight checks completed, the Aztec roared into life and the aeroplane taxied back along the tracks in the grass. Up they soared and the pilot took out his navigating equipment, handing Crawf the controls.

The Day Nationals Turned White

"Here, Crawf! Hang onto these. It's just like riding a bike!"

The New Zealander took hold of the control column before him and settled firmly back in his seat, a smile of achievement on his face.

BLEEEEEEP! BLEEEEEEP!

Crawf had never ridden a bike where the handlebars slid back toward the seat. He had inadvertently pulled the control column so far back that he was sending the plane into a steep climb and the stall warnings were screeching. The smile had disappeared!

Looking up, Colin calmly returned the plane to level flight. As the temporary novice pilot looked into the rear of the plane, he noted the Ni-Vanuatu passengers appeared to be the whitest nationals he had ever seen.

Washing the Angels' Feet

The 1975 Australasian Division Session was to be held in Marysville, Victoria, with representation from the islands among the delegates. These could travel by commercial airlines, or—as Colin did his sums—six delegates flown by the mission aeroplane would be a cost saving to the church.

He floated the idea with the Western Pacific Union Mission leaders and invited Colin Crawford, then teaching at Betikama in the Solomons, to fly with him.

"Would you come?"

"Yeah! I'll be in it!" was the response.

Later the New Zealander wondered why he had been so rash.

It was a long, slow flight, with cramped conditions and no toilet on board or meals served. On the other hand, the company would be genial and he would see places he had never seen before. So the deal was struck.

The flight began at Honiara with Crawf and a number of Solomon Island delegates as passengers. Constant banter between the Australian pilot and the New Zealand teacher kept the nationals amused as they flew to Santo to pick up the fifth passenger.

The final leg of the day's flight was to Tontouta—the main airport for Noumea—where the friendly and understanding Customs officer invited them to see him after they had paid a visit to the toilet.

The hospitality at Noumea was generous, even sacrificing an imported orange for each of the passengers to be consumed on the five-hour flight to Brisbane. However, before departure the next morning, the pilot gave a graphic account of the difficulty of toileting during the flight—so graphic that no-one ate their orange for fear of being "caught short."

It was a great relief to see Brisbane appear over the horizon. But the Australian Customs officer was neither friendly nor understanding. He demanded to see them before they visited the toilet.

After an enjoyable Sabbath in Brisbane, they took off for Cooranbong, flying south at 2000 feet (600 metres), which gave spectacular views of the Australian coastline. The island passengers were pleased to view the scenery but were most excited when Colin did a circuit over Avondale College before touching down on the Cooranbong airstrip. They had all heard of this special place called "Avondale." The overnight stay at Cooranbong was a highlight for each of them.

The next morning, as they were about to leave for Sydney, Colin said to Crawf, "You had better sit in front with me and hold the maps."

"Victor-Pappa-Pappa-Alpha-Zulu, track for Dee Why!" crackled Sydney Approach on the radio.

"Where's Dee Why?" asked Colin facetiously.

"Head for those trees!" responded Crawf, authoritatively.

Traffic control then directed them to head for the Sydney Harbour Bridge, much to the excitement of the national passengers who had heard of this Sydney icon. As the pilot lined up for the landing, the bridge emerged from the clouds, glowing in the sunlight.

After a short stopover in Sydney, they took off for Lilydale in Victoria, with Crawf in the co-pilot's seat once more. Colin asked him to keep a lookout for other aircraft, commenting, "They often fly with their lights on around here!"

In due course, Crawf spotted a bright object and drew the pilot's attention to it.

"Trust a New Zealander not to recognise a tin shed roof!" was the rejoinder accompanied by laughter from the passengers in the rear seats.

Soon they were over Lilydale Academy and Colin paddled the throttle to alert his student daughter of their arrival. Then the Lilydale airstrip came into view and after numerous calls for landing rights, the pilot was given permission to land. Lilydale had two runways. The shorter one appeared to have clumps of weeds growing on it. The longer one stretched flat and smooth, the ever-cautious pilot opting for the longer one.

Winchee

But only feet above the surface, Colin recognised duckweed—not a manicured surface. Nose up, they landed in inches of muddy water. The filthy fluid showered the plane, splattering splotches of mud over the windscreen.

Amid this surprise, the pilot's airmanship kept them from an unfortunate accident. Colin gunned the engines, ploughing through the duckweed and muddy water. As they slowed, a panicking man on a speeding Massey-Ferguson tractor pulled alongside and apologised profusely. They were "busy" and had the radio turned down so had failed to hear the pilot's calls.

As they exited the plane, they saw it was slime-covered right up to the tail emblem of the Three Angels. Land transport for the delegates was waiting, but the two Colins elected to stay back and—using buckets of clean water—flushed the many nooks and crannies on the plane.

Thus the pilot washed the Angels' feet.

Landing Rights and a Broken Wheel

In April 1976, Colin flew David Hay, the newly-appointed president of the Western Pacific Union Mission, secretary-treasurer Keith Hughes and education director Max Miller to Tarawa via Nauru to attend the annual meetings of the Gilbert and Ellice Islands Mission. They then flew to Abemama to visit the school, staying there over the Sabbath before flying on to Funafuti in the Ellice Islands.

As they approached these islands, Colin endeavoured to make contact with the Non-Directional Beacon (NDB)—without success!

Carefully, Colin and his passengers watched small atoll after small atoll pass by, before they finally spotted Funafuti. Thankfully, they spent the night visiting with the local worker and church members.

Next morning, all fuel tanks on the Aztec were filled for the direct six-hour flight to Vila. The necessary paperwork for the flight had been submitted more than a week before departure. About one hour into this flight, Colin contacted Vila Traffic Control via Nandi in Fiji, only to be told he had no permission to land at Vila. He decided to divert to Fiji but then was informed that the country was experiencing a cyclone.

His only option was to return to Funafuti. About 10 minutes out from Funafuti, he was informed that the authorities in Vila had discovered the paperwork and permission was now given for him to land.

After re-fuelling at Funafuti, Colin then flew to Vila, completing eight hours flying in the day when it should have only been a six-hour flight.

On arrival in Vila, the authorities apologised for the mix-up and congratulated Colin on completing the first direct flight between Funafuti and Vila. This achievement was given coverage that night on the local radio station, giving the Adventist mission excellent publicity.

Winchee

* * *

On another occasion, Colin flew with Gordon Lee and Keith Hughes to Vila to attend meetings, staying for a number of days. When it was time for them to return, they cleared Customs and Immigration, and fuelled the aeroplane for the four-and-a-half hour direct flight back to Honiara.

As Colin taxied the Aztec to the end of the runway in preparation for takeoff, he thought he heard a slight noise in the starboard wheel, which grew louder the further the plane went. He requested the Control Tower for permission to pull over onto the grass verge so he could check the scraping noise.

Permission given, Colin climbed under the aeroplane and noted that the brake disc was rubbing against the leg of the landing gear. At his request, Air New Hebrides sent an engineer to check the problem and declared it had to be changed.

With the permission of the control tower, the plane was returned slowly to the hanger where it was found that the wheel had cracked around the bolts that held the wheel together. If Colin had tried to take the wheel off, the whole thing could have collapsed.

The *J L Tucker* is ready at Funafuti, Ellice Islands,
for the six-hour flight to Vila, New Hebrides.

Landing Rights and a Broken Wheel

With no replacement wheels in the New Hebrides, one had to be ordered from Australia. This meant a delay of at least two days, so Gordon Lee caught a commercial flight back to Honiara, but Keith Hughes elected to stay with Colin in Vila. They booked into a cheap hotel to keep expenses down and, when the wheel was fitted, they enjoyed an uneventful flight back to Honiara.

Adventure on the Island of Fire

The Mt Yasur (Old Man) volcano on Tanna Island, southern Vanautu (New Hebrides), is the most accessible volcano in the world. The mountain peaks at 1184 feet (361 metres) above sea level and one may be driven in a four-wheel drive to within 500 feet (150 metres) of the crater rim.

On one visit to the island, Max Miller and Colin were taken by some of the local people to the car park at the base of the mountain and they made the steep climb to the crater rim. The volcano is constantly active with steam, smoke and—at times—molten rock tumbling down the mountain slopes. It is not unusual for molten rock to be thrust hundreds of feet into the air, falling back into the crater with a resounding thud. At such times, the crater climb is closed—for obvious reasons.

On the day the two missionaries made the climb, the volcano was active but not to that extreme level. They did note, however, that every three minutes or so the ground shook beneath their feet, and looking up, they saw dull red rocks of varying size tumbling down the slopes, rattling as they crashed into existing rocks on the bare slopes. Every so often, there was a booming sound like distant cannon fire. For someone of a nervous disposition, this could cause real fear but being of an adventurous character, Colin enjoyed the challenge and the spectacle.

Being in the tropics, it was hot enough but, with the added heat of the volcano and the stench of sulphur, the air tended to burn their lungs—and more so as they approached the rim of the crater. In the approach they heard half a dozen explosions, causing them to stop the climb and dodge falling molten rock.

Arriving at the rim, they looked down into the bubbling hot lava.

Colin noted that the activity would subside for a short time, then begin to build until the final explosion and expulsion of molten lava. Fortunately, they were not hit but looking behind them they were able to see the dull red of the ejected rocks rattling down the slopes.

The climb down from the rim was more frightening than the climb up. As the explosions continued, they would turn around and watch for more falling hot rocks.

Both men survived unscathed, as did the local people accompanying them. They could not help thinking what the earth might be like when the Lord returns and "the elements melt with fervent heat." A sobering thought.

Wes Guy: Aviation Mentor

Many individuals impacted the life of Colin Winch, but in the field of aviation, none more so than Wes Guy.

Born of missionary parents in 1922, Wes was educated at Box Hill Grammar School and later at Wesley College in Melbourne. By faith a Methodist, he met and married Pearl Fisher, a recently-baptised Seventh-day Adventist who bore him two sons.

A Royal Australian Air Force fighter pilot during the Korean War, Wes carried out 174 individual sorties in Meteor Jet Fighters. After successfully leading a squadron attack against a heavily-defended enemy Divisional Headquarters, he was awarded the Distinguished Flying Cross Medal, personally presented to him by Queen Elizabeth II when she visited Australia in 1954.

Wes was posted to Port Moresby in June, 1959, as the Examiner for Airmen with the Department of Civil Aviation. It was in this capacity that Colin came in close contact with this skilled pilot.

Though a nominal Christian, Wes was engaged in smoking, drinking and gambling, confessing to having little time for religion. He continually resisted the repeated invitations from Pearl to attend the Ela Beach Seventh-day Adventist Church with their family. Wes was a keen cricketer and this took precedence of a Saturday.

However, on one weekend, there was no cricket so Pearl invited him to attend the Bisiatabu camp-meeting. He reluctantly agreed, taking with him his transistor radio and ear clips so he could listen to the horse races. There Colin and Elwyn Martin introduced themselves to Wes and engaged him in conversation. Wes found them to be likeable and spent some time with them, temporarily forgetting the races.

Wes Guy: Aviation Mentor

Subsequently, Pastor Syd Stocken—a missionary who held a Private Pilot Licence—came into Wes' life and made repeated visits to his office. Under conviction that personal changes needed to be made, Wes contacted the Adventist Media Centre in Wahroonga, asking for Bible lessons to be sent to him. These he studied, as well as having continuing discussions with Syd, resulting in his baptism at Ela Beach Seventh-day Adventist Church on December 10, 1966, much to the delight of his family.

* * *

While on furlough in 1962, Colin had been working on his Commercial Pilot Licence and Flying Instructor Rating. On returning to Papua New Guinea late in the year, he still needed extra flying hours, so flew under the watchful eye of Keith Rose, the chief flying instructor at the South Pacific Aero Club in Port Moresby.

Finally, Mr Rose contacted Wes Guy, notifying him that Colin was ready for his final test. The first thing Wes noted was the record in Colin's log book that showed he had only completed 17 of the 20 flying hours required to qualify.

Wes Guy, pictured with his wife Pearl (left) and Melva (right), granted Colin his initial Instructor Rating in Port Moresby in 1962, and remains his mentor and dearest friend to this day.

Winchee

Nonetheless, the two airmen headed out to the parking bay where a Tiger Moth was standing.

In preparation for takeoff, Colin offered a prayer for safety. It was a new and somewhat strange experience for this secular Examiner of Airmen. The Tiger Moth was a plane Wes loved to fly, and Colin demonstrated his skill and knowledge as a pilot, having spent hours in Victoria flying the Tiger Moth owned by George Smith. Colin was given his Flying Instructor Rating and a bond of brotherhood was initiated between the two men.

While under appointment to Maprik in 1963, Colin needed further experience in flying under Papua New Guinea's hazardous conditions and was given permission by the officers of the Coral Sea Union Mission to fly as a temporary voluntary pilot with Stolair, a Port Moresby charter company. Though Colin was based at their branch in Daru, he was frequently in Port Moresby and in contact with Wes Guy and family.

* * *

In 1970, Wes was appointed operations director of Executive Air Services in Melbourne. By this time, he had been a member of the Adventist Church for three years and his expertise had not escaped the attention of the Australasian church leadership. A more positive attitude to the value of aviation ministry in the mission field had filtered down from the General Conference and the Australasian Division leaders were planning to further this form of outreach.

In 1975, Wes received a phone call from the Wahroonga church headquarters, inviting him to accept the position of Chief Pilot of the Australasian Division, hoping this responsibility would ensure the safety and standards of all mission pilots. He accepted this honorary position, leading out in training seminars and testing all mission pilots in Papua New Guinea and the Solomon Islands flying at that time. Having tested Colin in Honiara, Wes learned Colin was about to undertake a flight to Santo, Vila and Noumea, and he asked to join the flight. Colin was delighted for the company and the opportunity to swap aviation stories.

In 1976, Pastors Frame and Butler requested Wes to meet in

Wes Guy: Aviation Mentor

Wahroonga to discuss his interest in establishing a flying school under the umbrella of Avondale College, Cooranbong, the church's senior academic institution in Australia. For personal health reasons, Wes declined and recommended Colin for the responsibility.

Wes contacted Colin to notify him of the recommendation. Colin felt honoured and Melva was delighted at the prospect of returning to Australia to be with her family. They waited and waited, and were about to return from furlough to Honiara having heard nothing but rumours of the call, when Colin decided to visit the Division secretary to notify him of their departure.

"No, Brother Winch! Don't go! There is a call pending for you!" he was told.

Colin had loved his work in Honiara and was sad to leave it but saw the new responsibility of founding a flying school as a chance to train more pilots for the Lord's commission. However, Colin had allowed his Flying Instructor Rating to lapse and needed to re-activate it. So it was off to Melbourne where he again came under the tutelage of Wes Guy, before taking up his post at Cooranbong.

In 1980, Wes was contracted to Papua New Guinea's Department of Civil Aviation, which brought him into a "conflict of interest." Taking up his new role, he resigned his position as Chief Pilot of the Adventist flying program and recommended that Colin be appointed to the position. This took place on October 30, 1980. This new responsibility took Colin to Papua New Guinea, the Solomon Islands, Queensland, New South Wales, South Australia and Western Australia—anywhere within the South Pacific region where a pilot was flying a plane in connection with the mission of the Seventh-day Adventist Church.

However, Wes retained his interest in the aviation ministry of the church. On one occasion, Wes visited the airport at Cooranbong, dressed immaculately in a business suit and wishing to see where the proposed new airstrip was to be located. Colin had purchased a bright-yellow Ford Falcon in which he drove Wes to the western entrance of where the new strip would be formed. On entering the uncleared scrubby bush, the car became bogged and in spite of every effort remained immobile.

"Never mind, Col. I'll get out and push!" volunteered Wes. This

Winchee

he proceeded to do as Colin revved the motor, spinning the wheels. Instantly Wes was splattered with mud from head to foot. It was a measure of the man that he burst out laughing!

The Flying Instructor

Colin had flown aeroplanes for more than 6000 hours in Papua New Guinea, the Solomon Islands and throughout the Pacific when, in April, 1977, he was appointed as the inaugural Chief Flying Instructor for the Avondale College Flying School.

Retraining for his Flying Instructor Rating took place in Melbourne with Wes Guy and he was tested at Moorabbin by Gordon Howe, the Examiner of Airmen for the Department of Civil Aviation. Even though he passed this 30-minute test with flying colours, Colin still needed to build up instructional hours and was given permission to do so by the Seventh-day Adventist Church administrators.

He was accepted to voluntarily teach flying at Chieftan Aviation School in Bankstown, Sydney, for three days per week. He also was employed to voluntarily fly for Aeropelican Intercity Commuter Services out of Swansea, just south of Newcastle, where the Chief Flying Instructor was Stan Hone. Neither firm could believe their good fortune in snaring such an experienced pilot—and without cost!

The good will that was established paid dividends when Colin took over his new responsibilities at Cooranbong. Men such as Gordon Morris, who Colin began to instruct at Swansea, switched to Cooranbong to continue their training, as did a number of other Aeropelican students with the blessing of the kindly Stan Hone. Gordon Morris—a builder—not only put down a large tar-sealed apron in front of the Cooranbong hangers, but also brought two planes that he permitted the new flying school to lease at favourable rates.

By September 30, 1977, Colin had achieved his "Senior C" rating as an instructor and spent the month of October giving specialised

Winchee

instruction to Gill Davidson, later to become manager of the Avondale College Flying School. Lessons for students at Avondale College commenced on November 4, with Stan Hone holding the honorary position of Chief Flying Instructor until Colin had passed his "Level B" qualifications.

This he did on February 16, 1978, giving him full rights to take over the Flying School and to issue Pilot Licences on behalf of the Department of Civil Aviation. Pilots who trained under Colin and later became mission pilots included Max Mulligan, Peter Knopper, Reg Litster, David Bryce, Gordon Stafford, Ken Vogel, Graham Webster, Colin Dunn, Lionel Smith and Gary Clifford. Many more of his students completed their training but did not enter mission service.

Having himself received instruction from a number of flying instructors, Colin demanded a high standard of competence. Some of his methods were doubtless adopted from other instructors, but other methods were put in place as a result of the demands he had

Student pilot, Roger Millist, learns to fly with Colin in 1978.

The Flying Instructor

experienced while flying in New Guinea. These included methods to counteract emergency situations a pilot may encounter in mission flying.

Instruction included both theoretical and practical training. On registering, each student was given a Trial Instruction Flight that included handling the controls in order to get the feel of the plane while in the air. From this initial flight, each lesson gradually familiarised the student in the purposes and use of instruments and mechanisms, straight and level flying, climbing and descending, turning, stalling, circuits, forced landings, short-field takeoffs and landings, and other procedures.

When it came to the more advanced training, such as flying solely on instruments, Colin would place a hood over the trainee's head, allowing him or her to see only with restricted vision. It took away the trainee's view of the outside world and limited it to the aeroplane's instruments. It was important that the trainee implicitly follow the instruments' guidance.

To achieve straight and level flying demands a great deal of concentration and practice, perhaps the most difficult part of flying. Transferring into a controlled climb to a set altitude, then levelling off once more into straight and level flying was part of the learning process. Circuit training was important as it taught the fledgling pilot how to take off and land the aeroplane in various weather conditions, entering the approach to the runway and bringing the plane down gradually, lowering it onto the runway at the appropriate speed and runway position. Use of other senses other than sight is an important part of flying, particularly in landing. The ears become tuned to the sound of the motor and the estimate of the plane's speed through the air, all assisting in a safe return to earth.

Colin enjoyed working for five years at the Avondale Flying School with students of varying ages, helping them to fulfil their aviation dreams. But the call from church administrators to return to Papua New Guinea as an administrator, as well as to continue his work as Division Chief Pilot, was a challenge he could not resist.

Chief Pilot

Flying in Papua New Guinea is a hazardous occupation. High mountain peaks reach upward to the heavens, often with swirling storm clouds hiding them from the view of a novice pilot. Even the narrow passes through which a pilot may wish to cross from one airstrip to another may be dangerous due to up-draughts and down-draughts, sweeping any inexperienced pilot to an untimely death. Often covered with low-lying cloud or heavy fog, the swampy coastal lowlands are a hazard of a different nature.

Pilot error or mechanical failure—the unforgiving elements take their toll without regard for either. For this reason, mission pilots in training must be given the best and most rigorous instruction and stringent annual testing. Planes can be replaced, but human lives can not.

When Colin was appointed Chief Pilot of the Australasian Division in 1980, his role involved the care of as many as 30 church-affiliated pilots and 13 aeroplanes scattered throughout Papua New Guinea, the Solomon Islands and mainland Australia. He was also the denomination's liaison officer with the Department of Civil Aviation.

All of this was in addition to being Chief Flying Instructor at the Cooranbong Airport and—later in his career—in addition to being either secretary or president of the three island union missions at different times. Regardless of these heavy responsibilities, Colin found his work enjoyable, interesting and rewarding.

On an annual basis, he would check each pilot for competency, as well as conduct upgrading seminars. A check flight with a pilot consisted of simulated instrument flying, engine failures, forced landing practice and general unusual manoeuvres.

Usually, the pilot being tested was well aware that Colin would test him in some unexpected way and would keep an eye on his hand movements. The "emergency" must be presented as a surprise if it was to be realistic, so Colin would have to divert the pilot's attention by

Chief Pilot

pointing out some geographic feature that required him to look to his left. At that point Colin would switch a fuel tank off, pull out the fuel-mixture control, or turn the automatic pilot on which would make the plane react in some way the pilot wasn't expecting.

These "emergencies" were only simulated. A switched-off fuel tank or altered fuel mixture would cause the engine to cough, splutter and stop but Colin was careful to do this only if the plane was in gliding distance of an airfield. Should the pilot correctly diagnose the problem, he would quickly rectify what Colin had altered and the engine would burst back into life.

Pilot seminars would discuss aspects of pilot safety and other issues that would make Adventist aviation safer and more efficient. As a result, many of the minister–pilots developed into professional pilots with a real sense of pride in their abilities. Many men who held heavy responsibilities in the Seventh-day Adventist Church needed to be flown around the vast South Pacific Division, so the dependence on safe and skillful pilots was paramount.

"The Lord really blessed our efforts," Colin reflects on these years. "In

The Aztec at Batuna airstrip in the Marovo Lagoon in the Western Solomons. Left to right: Colin, Steve Fitzclarence — the sawmill and mission station manager — and John Banks, Western Pacific Union Mission Youth Director.

Winchee

my time as a pilot, I never had an accident—thank God. And during my time as Chief Pilot, under the blessing of God, we had no accidents at all."

Goroka Pilot's Seminar: (left to right) Ken Weslake, Aaron Jeffries, Colin Winch, Graham Wallace, Max Mulligan, Graham Webster, Gordon Stafford, Warren Price, Ken Vogel, Russ Gibbs.

Another Perspective:

As Chief Pilot, Colin was responsible for periodically checking the performance of all pilots flying for the Seventh-day Adventist Church in the South Pacific Division. This involved testing each pilot's ability to control an aeroplane in all kinds of flying configurations, such as short-field landings and "'dead stick" landings, which tested our ability to successfully land after a simulated engine failure. Another variation was a "'flapless landing," which meant that the landing speed was much faster than normal and used more of the already-short landing strip.

However, the test that freaked most of us out was the "stall and recovery" from an incipient spin. A pre-aerobatic check was carried out to ensure the aeroplane was fit and safe for the planned procedure. It was conducted so that the plane would safely recover from the test no less than 3000 feet (about 900 metres) above ground level.

This procedure involved pulling back on the elevator control, causing the nose of the plane to point steeply skyward. As the plane slowed, the stall warning would start to scream, warning the pilot that the plane was about to stall, which is a very unnerving experience!

When the aeroplane finally did stall, it would drop either wing. We had to wait to see which wing dropped, at which time we needed to "kick in" the opposite rudder to stop the incipient spin. This was a fairly docile experience at lower power settings, as the nose of the plane would gently drop away and point earthward making the recovery quite simple. The real test, however, came when we were asked to do this at full engine power. The results were anything but docile!

The most vivid recollection of a power stall and its subsequent recovery was conducted above the delta of the Markham River near Lae. All went well with the test until Colin requested that I demonstrate a full-power stall. I had not executed this manoeuvre in a Cessna 206 before, so I had dreaded this moment. Not fully knowing what to expect, I staunchly proceeded to execute the requested manoeuvre.

With the stall warning blaring, the motor screaming, the nerves jangling, the aeroplane seemed to flip onto its back and nose directly to the ground. I can still see the Markham River rushing up to meet us,

Winchee

feeling certain I was about to meet my Maker! At this point, I began to realise why my good friend Colin prayed such beautiful prayers. He always prayed as if he was about to meet his friend Jesus very soon.

As for the power stall, training kicked in and we survived the experience to continue to fly the Three Angels Message to the remote villages of Papua New Guinea.

—*Max Mulligan, retired mission pilot and pastor*

Family Memories and Reactions

Melva coped well as a missionary in her own right, the mother of a missionary family, as well as being the wife of a missionary pilot. Her training as a nurse gave opportunity to give repeated service as a midwife. Yet she admits to times of distress at some of the primitive conditions they were called to live in, particularly when she was expected to host visitors with no advance warning and inadequate supplies on hand.

At times, extreme loneliness, apprehension, and fear for her children and the safety of her husband affected her when living in remote mission outposts. There were times when Colin's absence caused sleepless nights. She would remain alert to every sound of the night, knowing that she and her children were the only white people in a community of nationals, some of whom were not favourably disposed to white faces. She was well aware there were those who desired to relieve Europeans of their private possessions.

According to her family, she would spend the night reading, with a stout "nulla nulla" fighting club under her bed and a starting pistol under her pillow. The pistol could not harm but it could frighten with its blast. One intruder experienced this as he endeavoured to make off with some of the family's possessions. Warned by the suspicious sounds, Melva fired the pistol—and the intruder left a trail of stolen goods in his haste to make his escape.

In their years in Lae, the Winch family inherited a cattle dog that decided it was her God-given responsibility to protect her mistress. Their home was surrounded by a barbed-wire six-foot (1.8-metre) high fence. If any caller came to the gate, the dog would immediately crouch

Winchee

between Melva's feet, staring with malevolent eyes at the visitor. Melva would advise the person not to endeavour to shake hands or touch her in any way as the dog would immediately attack.

On one occasion, an intruder was met by the dog and he decided that wounds incurred from the top strand of barbed wire were preferable to wounds from the gleaming fangs of the dog. He made a hasty exit!

* * *

In their early years of mission service, Melva had no direct contact with Colin when he was absent on patrol or in the air. She could listen in to the Civil Aviation Aircraft Control Frequencies for any information that would inform her of Colin's whereabouts and when he would complete his day's flying activities. Melva was able to tune her transistor radio into this network and listen to the pilots' conversations while in the air, while supervising the children's correspondence lessons.

When mission pilots were flying, they used a code to inform those at home of their intent. As the pilot flew over his home mission station, a single revving of the engine meant, "I'm just passing through." Two revs meant "I'm home. Please come to the airport and pick me up." Three revs meant "I'm landing with visitors on board. Please tidy up and come and get us!" This changed with the availability of a radio network covering all of Papua New Guinea and the Solomon Islands.

When the plane piloted by Laurie Shields crashed, killing him and three passengers, an air of foreboding descended on the wives of all mission pilots. Melva confessed to being nervous for some time after the incident, even though she knew Colin was an extremely careful pilot.

Each night Chris Winch prayed, " Please keep Daddy safe and help him not to crash." It was a big load for a little boy to carry into sleep.

However, Colin remained confident. He knew God was with him and, provided he did everything in his power to ensure safety, he was happy to leave the rest up to God. Colin constantly reminded himself and his fellow mission pilots of a traditional instructors' adage, "There are old pilots and bold pilots—but there are no old, bold pilots!"

* * *

Family Memories and Reactions

All four of Colin and Melva's children look back on their childhood years in the mission field as happy, carefree years. Nerolie wrote to her parents, saying, "When I see how other kids were raised here in Australia, I think I was very lucky to have such a diverse and well-travelled childhood. No regrets. Just great memories!"

All of them enjoyed making friends with the local mission children, seeing them as equals in every way. As they grew older and were located in centres where there were other expatriates, they appreciated interacting in play and school with children of their own ethnic background.

All the Winch children were active and adventuresome, sometimes featuring in risky activities. Cuts and bruises were frequent consequences, with both Nerolie and Chris suffering broken bones.

While living at Kainantu, Nerolie broke her arm at the inconvenient time when her Dad had flown overhead giving the signal that he needed to be picked up at the airstrip. A frazzled Melva took time to pick Colin up before taking Nerolie to the hospital to have her arm put in plaster.

The Winch family shares breakfast while living at Marprik: (left to right) Nerolie, Kerry, Colin, Carol, Chris, Melva.

Winchee

No lint was put under the plaster, so she lost some skin when the plaster was removed.

Chris was hit by a car in Port Moresby and suffered a spiral fracture of the tibia. His leg was plastered from foot to groin but when the family went swimming back in Kainantu, he simply could not resist the temptation to join them.

The result: a re-plastering of the leg at the Kainantu Hospital.

While staying at the Sepik Mission headquarters at Wewak, Nerolie nearly drowned at the local beach but Melva—heavily pregnant with Chris—jumped into the surf and saved her. Later in life, Nerolie nearly drowned a second time. This time Kerry and her friend went to the rescue, dragging her back to shore. They ignored her screams but once on dry land saw the reason for the screams. They had dragged Nerolie over a sharp piece of metal that had gashed her knee, opening a wound that required many stitches!

Kerry taught Nerolie to ride a bike by running behind her holding on to the dinker. At the mission office compound in Rabaul, there was a gently sloping road used by mission children as a thoroughfare for bikes. One day Nerolie was riding down the slope and Brod Lee—another mission kid—was riding up the slope. They played "chicken" with a resultant head-on crash. Nerolie's pride was all that was hurt, but Brod had a spoke penetrate his leg, a wound that caused him suffering for a considerable time.

* * *

Every member of the Winch family loved the water. Swinging out from a high point above the river and bombing into the water below is fun for any child, whether in the mission field or in the homeland. Hot, humid days made it particularly pleasurable. Sometimes on a Sabbath, the children would climb a tree hanging out over the water and "accidentally" fall in.

While living at Kainantu, a high tree swing provided hours of fun. One would climb the tree and a sibling would throw the swing up to the one in the tree who would leap out, catch the rope and enjoy a high, thrilling swing. One day, it was Nerolie's turn to climb the tree. The sibling pretended to throw the swing up to her and, anticipating

Family Memories and Reactions

the arrival of the swing, she leaped out. No swing arrived and the fall to the ground resulted in one bruised and cranky sister.

One of the favourite family water sports was "Gummying"—floating down the fast-flowing streams, dodging rocks and other hazards projecting from the swirling waters, while lying on inflated rubber tubes. It was exciting and had a high degree of danger for the inexperienced. The Lunga River at Honiara was highly regarded as good for "Gummying."

While enjoying a wild ride down the Busu River near Lae, Ida Millist was joining in with this family fun and almost lost her life, being trapped by a branch projecting from the fast-flowing stream. If it had not been for the immediate assistance of Colin, the day's fun may have ended in tragedy.

Linking Honiara to the airport, the high Bailey Bridge over the Lunga River provided another challenge to missionary kids—the challenge of leaping from various heights into the water below. It became a competition to see who dared to leap from the highest point and Chris took up the challenge on behalf of the Western Pacific Union Mission, yelling, "Victory to the WPUM!" as he plunged into the water from a height of 30 feet (about 9 metres).

Spending so much time in the water resulted in the children becoming strong swimmers. This proved true one furlough when Kerry entered her high school swimming carnival.

"I had swum a lot in the ocean and rivers but never in competition," she recalls. "I took off with my head down and swam as fast as I could only stopping for a breath at the end of each lap. I finished two laps ahead so I was put into every race that day. I was very excited I was able to do something better for once as I had struggled with being in such a big class in a big school and being very shy."

* * *

All the Winch children expressed deep love and respect for Melva. None of them were saints and, when they were disciplined, they knew it was well-deserved.

On one occasion, Chris had incurred the "wrath" of his mum and she gave chase to administer the appropriate punishment. The chase

Winchee

ended when Chris tripped over one of his sister's bikes and knocked out a tooth by falling on the bike's pedal. "Wrath" quickly dissipated and sympathy took over. For Chris, this was, "a picture of God—slow to anger and full of grace, mercy, and truth."

He also enjoyed sharing camping, fishing and flying trips with Colin. He noted his father's dependence on God, especially when about to take to the air. "I have taken this dependence on God into my own life," he says.

Kerry also remembers with pleasure the times she flew with her dad. If he had a spare seat in the plane, she would fly with him for as many as three days at a time. Colin also taught her how to eject the welfare bags through the open door of the plane.

"Dad would take me to help with a clothes bag drop," she explains. "He would take the door off the plane and strap me in with a secure shoulder harness, and show me how to get hold of the ear of the bag, which was bigger than me, and pull it up beside me in the doorway.

"We would fly to our destination and buzz the village so they would know we were about to drop a bag and they should stay clear. Then he would tell me when to push the bag out. It was cold, windy and exciting. We didn't always hit the mark but the people appreciated the clothes."

* * *

The Winch family lived in Australia from 1977 to 1981, during which time Colin established the flying school at Avondale College. As Chief Flying Instructor, he taught many prospective missionaries to fly and he was appointed Chief Pilot for the church in the Australian Division in 1979.

In 1982, a call came for Colin to return to mission service as secretary of the Papua New Guinea Union Mission, based in Lae. He and Melva wrestled with the call, knowing the fragmentation of the family may have dire consequences. Melva, particularly, was negative to the call but out of loyalty to her husband agreed to go.

Kerry and Nerolie seemed to handle separation from their parents without much trauma. However, even after two years living away from home at Lilydale Academy, Nerolie found the adjustment of living back

Family Memories and Reactions

in Australia difficult, particularly until she made new friends.

For Carol and Chris, it was a different story. Both were more emotional than their sisters and both developed negative attitudes to the situation that took their parents from them.

Speaking of her thinking at the time, Carol wrote:

> I often felt that the missionaries were doing the work of the church first, then serving God second; and finally the family was last. I even began to blame God for my hurts. What a saint my mum is. It must have worried her being alone so many times as my dad was absent on "God's work."
>
> There were times when I even questioned the "good" that the church was doing. I saw native kids in Highland villages, cold and freezing with green snot running down from their noses, in skimpy white man's clothes, shivering as they washed themselves with cakes of sunlight soap in freezing mountain streams. To me, as a child, it didn't make sense. Pig fat was a better option. At least they were warmer!

The family sadly farewells Melva, Carol and Colin as they prepare to take off from Cooronbong for Lae, Papua New Guinea, in 1982.

Winchee

I didn't realise the impact the break from my family had on me until later years. I was in a small group and an old missionary from another church was talking about doing God's work and how he sent all his children back to Britain at a young age, when I interrupted him. "You call that God's work! How dare you sit there and call that God's work! Your first and foremost missionary work is to your family. Don't you dare call that missionary work!"

I sobbed and sobbed. The meeting had to be closed because of me. I was inconsolable, embarrassed and distraught. I know my mum and dad did what they thought best—but there are so many dysfunctional missionary kids out there!

Chris also went through a personal crisis due to his parents' absence:

I recall standing, stunned, on the tarmac of the Cooranbong airport as my whole support structure flew away and disappeared into the sky. Little did I realise how much I really needed them over the next couple of years. But we were never to be that family unit again that I so desperately craved. I started to blame, first, my dad for having left. God was also in my targets. After all, was it not mission service that had taken my family away from me?

The next seven years saw Chris seek to solve his loneliness in substance abuse until a series of accidents caused him to take a radical look at his life and renew his commitment to Jesus Christ

As he recorded his story, the tears flowed. Tears also flowed down the faces of Colin and Melva, and they want these stories recorded because they are aware of the hurts held in the hearts of many missionary families who faced similar decisions.

However, there were other—more positive—effects in the Winch family. Kerry graduated as a nurse from Sydney Adventist Hospital and returned to Papua New Guinea as a missionary in her own right. With some of her classmates, she served as a nurse at Sopas Hospital.

"It's a Miracle"

The usual tropical afternoon storms not having presented themselves, Colin sat in the pilot's seat basking in the glory of the scenery below. He had placed the twin-engine aeroplane on autopilot as they followed the northeast coast of Bougainville on course to Rabaul.

On board was Milton, who had been principal of the Rumba Central School, and his wife Betty, who were transferring to Madana Central School in Papua. Accompanied by their two large dogs in the rear cargo compartment, the MacFarlanes elected to sit on the centre seats where the dogs could see them and be easily attended to should they become stressed. This left the seemingly vacant co-pilot's seat—as Colin was wont to say—for his guardian angel.

They had taken off from Aropa International Airport, which served the township of Kieta, and climbed to an altitude of 7500 feet (2200 metres). Now the plane was on autopilot, Colin had little to do but talk to his passengers, while keeping an eye out for other aircraft. They could see Mount Bagana with a horsetail-shaped plume of smoke issuing from its crater. This was an exceptional view as the mountain is normally obscured from view by cloud.

The *J L Tucker* soon passed over the Buka Non-Directional Beacon and, at the northwest end of Bougainville, Colin set course for Rabaul. One hour later, they were passing over the active volcano of Matupit on final approach to Rabaul Airport.

Colin refuelled the plane and checked the oil in both engines, while the MacFarlanes took their dogs for a walk before re-boarding for the two-hour flight to Lae on mainland New Guinea.

In the final 30 minutes of this segment of the trip, Colin noticed a slight vibration in the airframe of the aeroplane. Wondering as to the cause, he checked the plane's instruments.

To his shock and consternation the port (left-hand) engine's oil-pressure gauge showed no pressure, indicating a major problem. There was no time to alert the MacFarlanes. Immediately he swung

Winchee

into action, closing the engine down, feathering the prop.

Milton noted that the prop was stopping spinning. He let out a roar, "What are you doing, Winchee?"

"Just a moment, Milt, while I complete closing down this engine. Then I will explain it to you."

Colin advised Lae Control Tower that he had closed down the port engine due to no oil pressure and was cleared to make a straight-in approach to the runway. Milton and Betty heard the two-way conversation with the tower and became understandably quiet. They heard the tower authorities giving instructions to other aircraft approaching Lae to hold clear as there was an aircraft on an emergency straight-in approach. The MacFarlanes knew they were on this aircraft. They were part of the emergency!

To add to Milton and Betty's tension, they could see numerous flashing beacons as fire engines and ambulances positioned themselves in preparation for immediate action should the aeroplane crash and burst into flames. Colin was fully aware of preparations being made on the ground for the landing. But his mind and energy were fully directed to what had to be done to land the plane safely.

Landing on one engine was not a problem. The problem was that the port engine also controlled the mechanism for lowering the landing gear. Having shut down this engine, Colin now had to manually pump down the landing gear with one hand, while he flew the plane with the other.

With adrenalin flowing, he began the task. At least 60 pumps of the lever would be required. Up and down, he pumped, up and down, up and down, with each action the task became more difficult as pressure built up on the mechanism. Up and down, up and down—until eventually the three lights on the instrument panel indicated the landing gear was down.

The plane touched down without incident and was cleared to taxi to the Macair Maintenance Facility. Bowing his head, Colin thanked their heavenly Father for the safe landing, to which the MacFarlanes uttered a hearty "Amen." Two very relieved passengers disembarked, collected their dogs and headed for the terminal.

As soon as Colin alighted from the plane, he noticed that under the

"It's a Miracle"

left wing behind the engine and underneath the fuselage was covered with oil, yet they had smelled nothing while they were flying. He shuddered when he realised the oil coming from the engine must have been flowing very close to the hot exhaust pipe.

Why had the engine not caught on fire earlier in the flight, because the oil had obviously been leaking for some time? And if he had not switched off the engine when he did, the engine would have blown up and he and his passengers would likely have perished in the resulting fire!

The Macair chief engineer walked across the tarmac and interrupted Colin's silent prayer of thanks. When he saw the copious amount of oil under the fuselage, he filled the air with colourful expletives.

Looking at Colin, he exclaimed, "You're a lucky bugger!" Shaking his head, he circled the aeroplane and the expletives continued.

"I'll get one of the engineers to have a look at it straight away. You can watch if you like."

Colin unloaded the MacFarlanes' luggage and the plane was pulled into the hanger. The engineer removed the engine's cowls and started an unusual and interesting chain of events.

The engineer checked the oil stick. It was dry.

"That can't be right!" he muttered. So he checked it again. It came up dry again. A few expletives. "Did you hear the engine rattling before you closed it down?"

Colin indicated there had been no unusual noise, only a slight vibration that he felt coming through the fuselage and the pilot's seat.

"I'll undo the drain plug and see if there is any oil left."

There was just one quart (about 1 litre) of oil left in the engine. These Lycoming engines run with 12 quarts and should never be allowed to get below 10 quarts. He took out the spark plugs and turned the propeller by hand. No noise!

"You have done in your engine for sure!" the engineer concluded. "These engines will not run with less than three quarts of oil. I'll take out the oil filter and cut it up and show you all the metal it trapped. You will need to get another engine. This one is done for. Can't make out why it's not making any noise when I turn it though!"

Silently, Colin prayed. "Please, Lord. The aircraft is just a few months

Winchee

old. It is just run in. We cannot afford another engine. We need this machine to extend Your work. We need a miracle! Dear Jesus, please give us a miracle!"

The engineer gripped the filter in a vice and, taking a mean-looking knife, he slit the heavy innards and opened them out along the bench. "Come close," he invited, "and I will show you all the metal from your damaged engine . . . That's funny! There is nothing here! It's as clean as a whistle! How can that be?"

He walked across to the aeroplane with furrowed brow and put the plugs and a new oil filter back in. He asked some of the national aircraft cleaners to wash the engine and fuselage clean, then he filled the engine with new oil. This done, he asked Colin to start the engine and run it for about five minutes.

When the engine was again closed down he checked for leaks. There were none! He tied small plastic bags over all the engine vents and overflow tubing and asked Colin to fly the plane around the circuit a couple of times. Still no leaks!

As a final test, he asked Colin to fly it again, but this time to climb to 8000 feet (2400 metres)—the altitude the plane flew at from Rabaul to Lae. Colin was to stay at this elevation for 30 minutes.

That did it! On landing, one of the plastic bags was bloated with oil. On examination, it was found that the seal that prevents engine oil coming from the engine sump had not been pressed home properly when the engine was first manufactured. Somewhere between Rabaul and the Vitiaz Strait, the seal had started to leak, causing almost all the oil from the engine to be pumped overboard.

The engineer looked straight at Colin and said, "It's a miracle!"

That engine continued to operate for its full life with no further problems.

Flying With an Angel

It was a stormy April night in 1976 when Colin received an emergency call to fly an injured Tongan man from Santo (New Hebrides) to Noumea (New Caledonia). With long-range fuel tanks, it was a flight the *J L Tucker* was capable of making.

The accident victim had been riding his motorcycle at speed when he collided with a Jeep, also travelling at speed. The impact propelled the Tongan through the air, sustaining life-threatening injuries to many parts of his body.

Realising the medical facilities at the Santo French Hospital were inadequate to handle such a serious case, the chief surgeon requested the emergency flight to the better-equipped hospital in Noumea. There could be no delay as a life was at stake, so a diminutive French nun was entrusted to monitor the patient's needs during the flight.

The seats were removed from the plane to make room for the stretcher carrying the semi-conscious patient. Colin indicated to the nun that she occupy the co-pilot's seat, but she declined, insisting in broken English that she sit on the floor alongside her patient. Colin rigged up seatbelts to ensure her safety and climbed into the pilot's seat.

It was his habit to pray before takeoff, but not being fluent in the French language, indicated his intention by signs to the French Sister who bowed her head and crossed herself in true Catholic fashion.

"Dear Heavenly Father," Colin prayed, "please give us a safe flight tonight. Guide Sister Angelique as she ministers to her patient. Bear us up and bring us safely through the storms ahead to a safe landing in Noumea. In Jesus' name, Amen!"

On clearing for takeoff, Colin was advised by the control tower to be

Winchee

prepared for a stormy flight. He was to fly through the Inter-Tropical Emergence Zone where northwest and southeast trade winds meet, causing accumulation of Cumulonimbus storm clouds inside of which violent turbulence could occur.

The Aztec lifted into the smooth night air and Colin headed on direct track to Tontuta, the international airport for Noumea. Lightning could be seen lighting up the clouds ahead, so Colin notified the diminutive nun that she should keep her seat belts tightly strapped and secure her medical case. The patient was restlessly throwing himself from side to side, demanding her full attention.

Then the plane was in the cloud. The turbulence was horrific. The Aztec was being shaken like a dog shakes a rat. One minute a great column of rising air thrust the plane aloft at 5000 feet (1500 metres) per minute, only to be followed by a down-draught that sent the bucking plane earthwards at 5000 feet per minute.

Though Colin was experienced in flying in rough weather, he had never experienced anything like these extreme conditions. Even though he attempted to arrest the descent by applying full power, it was to no avail. For some 30 minutes, the plane and its occupants were at the mercy of the elements, plunging up and down like a bare-back rider in a giant rodeo.

Colin grimly hung on to the vibrating controls, while Angelique continued the care of her patient in these incredible circumstances. When she dared to loosen her seat belt in order to adjust the intravenous drip, she was flung from side to side. On more than one occasion, her medical case had risen from the floor, floated weightlessly around, then crashed down again.

Lightning was forking all around the aeroplane and, inside the cabin, an eerie blu-ish light brightened the cockpit. The whole atmosphere was electric, on occasions temporarily blinding the pilot. After one lightning flash, Colin noticed the plane's instruments had become blurry, as had the chart lying on his lap. He rubbed his eyes but to no effect.

"O please, Lord, not my eyes!" he prayed. "Not now, Lord!"

Moving his hands to touch the instrument panel, Colin's finger made a smear. He touched the chart with the same result. It was blood! The patient was coughing up a fine spray of blood.

Flying With an Angel

Colin turned to speak to Angelique and noted that the sister's dazzling white uniform was now soiled with smears of blood.

"How is your patient?" Colin asked.

"Not veeery good!" was the reply. "Ve must geeet to the 'ospital queeeekly!"

At that moment, amid the roar of the storm and the vibrating and plunging of the plane, Colin sensed someone was seated in the co-pilot's seat. The impression was so strong he was forced to take his eyes of the instrument panel and look toward the vacant seat. Regardless of the buffeting of the storm, an inner peace pervaded his mind. He sensed there were four people aboard that aeroplane and all would be well.

Minutes later, the Aztec burst out of the edge of the storm and entered smooth, clear air. The sky was brilliant with stars and ahead could be seen the lights of the northeast coast of New Caledonia.

But a decision had to be made. Should he land at Tontuta and subject the patient to a 40-mile (65-kilometre) drive to the hospital? Or should he land at Magenta, an airstrip in Noumea within a mile of the hospital?

The condition of the patient determined the decision. He notified Tontuta control tower that he would proceed directly to Magenta. The controller advised that this would not be possible. As this was an international flight, Customs, Immigration and Health would have to be cleared at Tontuta.

Colin made a captain's decision. The Tongan's health was failing fast, so he insisted he would land at Magenta. Somewhat grudgingly, the controller cleared the plane to land at Magenta where an ambulance would be waiting on the tarmac. Colin landed the plane safely despite crosswinds gusting up to 25 knots (45 kilometres per hour) and taxied to the waiting ambulance.

Having loaded her patient into the vehicle, Angelique turned to Colin and said, "Tonight God flew with us, did He not?"

"Yes, Angelique. He most certainly did!"

The blood-smeared nun joined her patient in the ambulance and was gone.

Colin returned to the bloodied Aztec and prepared to secure it for the night. As he stood on the wing, he heard a distant rumble of thunder. Looking in the direction of his flight, he could see lightning still playing

Winchee

its fantastic dance among the towering clouds. Stretching weary back muscles and looking heavenward to the blazing stars, he offered a short prayer.

"Thank you, Lord, for bringing us safely through! And Lord, thanks, for tonight I flew with an angel!"

Then he remembered Angelique. "Lord! Make that two angels!"

Afterword

As one reads the story of Colin and Melva Winch, one realises anew that God cares for all people but has a special interest in His missionaries. While Colin and Melva did not pioneer the work of the Seventh-day Adventist Church in Papua New Guinea, Colin and Len Barnard, with no early encouragement from the denomination's leaders, did pioneer the work of Adventist aviation, demonstrating that, with the careful and prayerful use of aeroplanes, work could be achieved at a fraction of the time and with greater efficiency than it took foot-slogging through crocodile-infested swamps or leech-infested tropical jungles. Mission boats and foot patrols still had their place and both men shared in these activities but, in part as a result of the flying program they pioneered, the Advent message spread like a wildfire through Papua New Guinea and the Pacific.

Encouraged by an old German church member's often repeated "Vun day you vill be a meesionary," Colin dreamed an ever-expanding dream of flying aeroplanes to hasten the work of pushing back the frontiers of fear, ignorance and superstition in lands where the powers of Satan were daily demonstrated. He dreamed a dream of he and Melva using their training as nurses to mend broken bodies wounded in inter-tribal battles, of healing tropical diseases with appropriate medication, of treating those afflicted with leprosy so they might have the opportunity of returning to village life, of reducing the rate of infant mortality, of providing emergency life-saving flights to those in need of urgent specialised treatment.

Colin dreamed a dream of establishing new landing strips on mountain slopes and in swampy jungles, giving quick access to nationals working for their own people or being placed in remote areas where white expatriates would be unwelcome. Colin dreamed a dream of training other men and women to become skilled pilots in the work of spreading the gospel.

Now as he looks back over his life, he is able to thank God for dreams

Afterword

that have been brought to fruition under the blessing of the Almighty, and with the support of his loving wife.

"We have had a wonderful life!" he reflects.

WHEN GOD CALLS, EXPECT ADVENTURE

LESTER HAWKES with BRAD WATSON

From coral-fringed Papua to the incredible Highlands of New Guinea and remote Pitcairn Island . . .

Lester and Freda Hawkes worked tirelessly to share the love of God as medical missionaries.

Answering God's call really does lead to incredible adventure.

Available NOW at your friendly Adventist Book Centre